The Colorful Path: Towards Lasting Relationship and Love

RACHAEL F. AFOLABI

Copyright © 2018 by Rachael F. Afolabi

All rights reserved. This book or any portion thereof may not be reproduced or used in any manner whatsoever without the express written permission of the publisher except for the use of brief quotations in a book review.

Contents

Introduction 1

Chapter 1: Who am I? 11

Chapter 2: A Memoir or a Self-Help Book? 16

Chapter 3: Lessons Learned 23

    You've Got to Love You 25

    Irreconcilable Differences 26

    Pressure 27

    Make Hay While the Sun Shines 29

    Values Must Align 31

    Conflicts 36

Chapter 4: Do Not Settle for Less 39

Chapter 5: Three Must-Have Connection 45

    Emotional Connection 45

    Intellectual Compatibility 48

    Spiritual Connection 50

Chapter 6: Is There a Perfect Marriage? 53

    Work Work Work Work Work Work 54

Chapter 7: What We Learned in Biology Class 57

    Mutualistic Symbiotic Relationship 58

    Commensalistic Relationship 59

    Parasitic Relationship 59

    Becoming Whole 61

    It's the Most Important Decision *Ever* 62

CHAPTER 8: Be Careful of Wolves in Sheep's Clothing 66

When I Ended It 73

A Testimony in Progress 78

Chapter 9: My Love and Hate Relationship with African Men 86

My Wish Above All 90

Chapter 10: The Four Pillars of Marriage 91

Respect 93

Understanding 96

Forgiveness 98

Sacrifice 99

Chapter 11: A Note from Me to You 102

Why Do Marriages Fail 104

Chapter 12: Some Favorites Posts from My Blog 111

All You Need is Love and Then Some 111

Why Am I Still Single? 115

Ìwà lẹwà (Character is Beauty) 117

When the Thrill is Gone 122

When the Going Gets Tough 126

The Best Quote I've Ever Heard About Love 131

A Letter to Her Lover: Love is Not Enough 133

I'm Choosing Love, Warmth in the Arms of My Lover and
Matrimonial Bliss 136

What Makes Marriage Worth It? 140

The Helpmate: For Singles and Married 144

Chapter 13: Hey Ladies! Let's Talk Submission. 147

Conclusion 150

Dedication:

To my mother Grace Olufunke Olaniyan –

I finally wrote my own book.

INTRODUCTION

A very depressing conversation I had with a dear friend led to the conviction to complete and publish this book. Although, I began writing this book two years ago, I could not complete it due to certain events that took place in my life that led to the alteration of some of the knowledge I thought I had about marriage and relationships. These experiences revealed just how much more I needed to know. As a result, I have had to modify the book to include lessons I've learned over the last couple of years. I have acquired more knowledge which have increased my confidence to the level that I finally feel insightful enough to give this book the writing it deserves.

While every relationship is unique and different, there are

general guidelines and rules that apply. In spite of all the numerous books on relationships and marriage from some of the most brilliant brains in the world, people still manage to simply suck at it. If you picked up this book, I believe it must be because there is a real need you believe it could satisfy or because you just wanted to abate your curiosity. Whatever the motivation for reading this book, I see no reason to sugarcoat my words. If this book hits home with just a handful of people, then my assignment is fulfilled.

You don't need me to spell it out to you; marriage is a failing institution! We have the data and statistics to prove that. *PEW Research* states that 25% of millennials will never get married. While 41% of the remaining 75% who are likely to get married will end up divorcing if the US divorce statistics are correct. Yet I was sad to hear my friend say, "People don't want marriage." Particularly, young people. Here was another young person sharing a pessimistic assessment of marriage, I was disheartened. But his statement was not at all surprising.

It seemed as though this rising divorce and failed marriage epidemic is an easier pill to swallow when we read about it online or see it on the news. For one, it's a frequent occurrence among Hollywood celebrities. I completely lost faith in celebrity marriages when *Brangelina* broke up. They seemed so in love. Some few months back when it was reported that Channing Tatum and his wife also got a divorce, my heart broke to pieces, but the surprise element was gone. I won't be shocked if by the time this book is published, some other Hollywood power couple have decided they've had enough of this institution called marriage.

But whether on television or in person, divorce is a bitter pill. When we are confronted with it face to face, it becomes more difficult to digest. Such was the conversation I had with my friend. Here we are, two young individuals with plans to take the plunge into holy matrimony someday, hopefully soon. But if we are being completely honest with ourselves, we know that there is no guarantee that our marriage will work or that it will stand the test of time.

While divorce is clearly the most overt proof of the failure of a marriage, many married couples can attest to the fact that it is unfortunately not the only failure that can befall a marriage. Some couples choose to remain together, but not necessarily happily.

I used to consider myself a hopeless romantic. I loved the idea of two individuals coming together to live happily ever after. My teenage years were filled with reading romance novels (Mills & Boon, Harlequin, Silhouette, etc.), you name it, I read them all. I hid some of the scandalous covers carefully from my parents. It was shocking to see some of the intimate embraces on the covers of those books. This was only a few years back, to see how much more exposed teenagers today are to even more sexualized images on television and online bothers me a little. But if there was one thing reading romance novels taught me, it was the truth that the human imagination is so wide and wild. Reading those books incited me to stretch my own imagination as well.

So, in addition to reading romance novels, I would write mine and share them with peers. Like all of the books I gorged on, mine always ended with a happily ever after as well. Naturally, an older version of myself was the heroine in all of these stories and whoever my current crush was at the time became the Prince Charming.

But as an adult, I have come to realize that real humans do not follow the script as characters do. Real humans haven't quite imbibed the "happily ever after" theory yet as our romance heroes and heroines have. Consequently, I have learned to be more realistic than hopeless. But I have not stopped being a romantic.

Being the romantic that I am, I was quick to reject the assertion that people no longer wanted marriage. My friend's statement did not sit well with my romantic sensibilities. I mentioned some of our friends who have recently tied the knot and those who have picked out a wedding date. These couples certainly invalidated his theory, I argued.

After much back and forth, we settled on a position we could both agree on. It is not that young people don't want marriage, we want marriage, we want love, we want romance, we want that! What we don't want is the responsibility that comes with it.

There are a few points I am going to mention throughout this book that you are probably already aware of but bear with me, overtime I have learned there's power in repetition. So, although some of these things have been said before, it really sinks into our minds when they are repeated. One of them I mentioned earlier when I stated that marriage is a failing institution. Another one is that this generation (Younger Generation X, Millennials, Generation Z) have a completely different set of values from previous generations. While we may point to the marriages of our grandparents and in some cases our parents as proofs that marriages do succeed, we must realize that the values that governed their lives are different from those that govern ours. Their marriages were based on inter-dependability (I wash your back, you wash mine). But this generation has highly individualistic mindsets (you do you, I do me). The problem is that we are trying to make marriage happen under this premise. What ends up happening in many cases is cohabitation, not marriage. Although, we have the certificate and wedding pictures as evidence that we got married, there is no actual marrying. Frankly, marriage cannot survive with self-centered ideologies. However, we still want the beauty that marriage represents (everlasting love, soulmate, to love and to hold, forsaking all others...) Well, it comes with a price!

Most of my write-ups about love and relationships ring of pessimism rather than the positivism and delight we imagine when we think about love. In fact, a reader once termed me a "pessimistic sojourner." A very felicitous description I'll say. Not that my writing painted a gloomy picture of love and marriage, on the contrary, its true intention was to demonstrate that love - that beautiful element that we all desire to have is attainable, but not without some efforts, preparations and perseverance.

This love I am referring to is not to be mistaken with a strong feeling, or a deep romantic or sexual attraction. Although, feelings and attractions could be the starting point of this love. After all, we are not mere robots or mechanical beings devoid of emotions. Attraction, desire, and affection are all very important, but it does not end there.

When I use the word love I am referring to something more seasoned and refined. Much like gold, it has passed through a fiery experience to be purified and proven to be genuine. This love is not something that we stumble upon or fall into. I once wrote, "I fell in love" is one of the biggest flim-flams we ever invented.

This love is a journey. It takes several years of being together as a couple to truly test its realness. The durability of a marriage is one of the testaments to the love the couple share. Seeing how the lifespan of marriages are dwindling in this generation, I dare say, what we have is a love problem. Are you willing to pay the price?

I find it fascinating how we anticipate that success comes with much effort and perseverance. We expect that those who ultimately become successful in life are those who have worked hard and prepared for it. But when it comes to love and marriage, we propose a different set of rules. Some of us imagine it will all just fall on our laps like leaves fall from trees, effortlessly. Love is arguably the apex of marriage. Yet we define it as feelings and emotions. This does not add up. If love was merely a feeling it would not be worth all the joy and misery it gives. Yes, love gives much joy and equally much misery.

The reality is that there is a price to love. It's not all roses, white sheets, and champagne. Romance novels, movies, and love songs do not come close to giving us the full picture. They are instead a painful reminder of the failure marriages have become, by being everything we aspire toward, but fail to attain. We fall short of faithfulness, happiness, complete devotion, and *forever*, because they come with a high price tag.

This generation more than past generations have access to a myriad of information (good, bad, wrong, right, ugly, moral and immoral). This information presents us with options. We have a vast array of alternatives for how we choose to live how lives.

Many lifestyles are permissible (sologamy, LGBTQ, cohabitation, single parenthood). With this many options, we might think the value of heterosexual marriage has decreased. But it's quite the opposite. If anything, the value of a good heterosexual marriage has drastically increased. How come? Rarity gives value to an object. Think of antiques and precious stones; their rarity makes them valuable and costly. A good heterosexual marriage is a rare commodity these days; it is so hard to come by. The way people desire precious stones, they long for a good marriage! This reverts back to my earlier statement; people want marriage, but not the price that comes with it. As do every good thing in life, love has a price tag. The question, the burning question then is, are we willing to pay the price for love? The sort that lasts forever, like diamonds last forever? Then the payment starts right now.

This book is for all and sundry, single, married, divorced or in a relationship. If you're single, I urge you to take the opportunity to get some basic knowledge before you launch into the deep waters of marriage. If you're married, I encourage you to make it work or make it stronger. If you are in a relationship, I challenge you to let this book serve as a mirror of reflection. If you are divorced, I admonish you; this book may give you a clearer picture of where things went wrong.

Times have indeed changed and so must our approach to marriage. It is no longer feasible to rely on the methods that older generations used in choosing life partners to decide who we want to spend the rest of our lives with in this day and age. It's like putting new wine in an old wineskin, it won't work. Different sets of rules apply. But before I continue, allow me to introduce myself and the source of information you're about to receive. I believe source is very important. As late Dr. Myles Munroe used to say, source determines the integrity of a message.

RACHAEL F. AFOLABI

CHAPTER 1: WHO AM I?

Who is this young woman, does she have any qualifications, and why should I even pay attention to her? Are questions you are probably asking if you've made it this far already. And that's okay; I asked myself these very questions when I committed myself (time, resources, experiences) to start writing and speaking about relationships and marriage.

I'm a twenty-something young unmarried woman, so why should anyone pay attention to me? This was the reason I tarried until I had completed a college education before launching my relationship blog, and until I have acquired a master's degree before uploading my first relationship vlog. Although, they were both desires I have wanted to **fulfill** since I was a teenager, I did not move forward because I believed that credibility is the soul of a writer.

I was too young, and the discipline of writing is to be taken seriously. Particularly when addressing a sensitive subject like marriage. I believe having an education adds to one's respectability and credibility, and I needed those so desperately because I wanted to address topics and issues surrounding marriage.

The general belief is that only married folks have the right to talk about these things and if you were unmarried, you should at least have some serious experiences. But age was not in my favor, and neither have I ever been married nor divorced. I was an easy prey for any critic who was looking to attack my viewpoint on these issues or, so I thought.

Interestingly, many of the feedbacks I have received about my blog posts on relationships are that *I come across as someone who is very experienced*. Readers who do not know me personally have assumed I am married, some that I am divorced, and others that I am a woman in my thirties with lots of experiences when it comes to relationships. But I was only twenty-three when I started writing about relationships. And if not for my inhibitions about the way of the world, I would have started at a much younger age.

But I have come to realize that people will criticize you if they so choose. Even if you were Oprah or Joyce Meyer, people would still censure you if they so please. So, you might as well go for it. Whatever *it* is. In my case, writing and speaking about relationships and marriage.

Writing about relationships was strongly imprinted on my heart. It broke my heart into pieces every single time I saw people I knew fail at marriage. I felt a strong need to do something, anything. Knowing I am gifted in writing and speaking, the logical conclusion was to speak out loud and write volumes. And what better topics to write about, other than the ones that most concerned me and indeed the broken hearted?

I just couldn't wait until I was old enough, married or experienced enough to start being vocal about these things, because the more I wait, the more marriages will fall apart! Couples are not waiting for me to grow old before they decide to sign divorce papers. Neither are young folks waiting for me to be experienced before they say "I do" to the wrong person. So why hesitate when there is a slight possibility that what I have to say is what someone out there needs to hear to make the right decision?

If there is any question as to where I get my ideas from, I'll say years of learning from my family. I have great role models in my parents who have been happily married for close to thirty years now. I also learn from books, seminars, speakers, and ministers. I realize that professing that I read a lot of books **will** make me come across as an intellectual person, but truth be told, I find many inspirational/motivational/self-help books incredibly boring, like I did most of my college textbooks. I had rather watch a Korean drama than read a book. Even though the storyline may not be realistic, it at least ends happily. But I do read and encourage people to read, because quite frankly, reading is good for **us** and there are wisdoms that can only be expressed through written words. Besides, we do not read these kinds of book for fun but for much-needed knowledge. I wouldn't be the person I am today without books; they continue to transform every aspect of my life.

Of late, I have stopped watching as much Korean dramas and started reading more books. One of the reasons being, in order for me to be a good writer, I need to make reading a lifestyle. Besides, let's face it, Korean dramas are mostly entertainment, and so are all other soap operas and TV shows. We pick one or two tidbits from them sometimes, but that's nothing compared to the knowledge we gain from reading.

As for experiences, I have had my own fair share of failed relationships, about one or two. I find those more than sufficient. I don't need to have gone through several series of scarring encounters to be able to write a good book about relationships. But experience they say is the best teacher. Therefore, I borrow and learn from the experiences of those I have been privileged to encounter. I do not need to go through the harrowing and grotesque experience of divorce to know it is a devastating and life-altering event that I want no part of.

If these answers are not sufficient, then, I get my inspiration from above. Many of what I write, come from a very deep and spiritual place. Considering my mentioned limitations (young, not married, not experienced), I can only attribute my passion for marriage to God. Writing about relationships and marriage is a mission that has been laid in my heart, something I'll refer to as a calling. I hope everyone will be open-minded about this book and give it a compulsive read.

CHAPTER 2: A MEMOIR OR A SELF-HELP BOOK?

When I received the inspiration to write this book, I did not know what genre it was going to conform to, whether a memoir, an inspirational, motivational or self-help book. However, I knew I had to include a personal narrative. I believe my story can really help someone, even if my life does not typify that of many people.

    I was born and raised in Lagos city, Nigeria, to parents who were "born again" Christians. In fact, my father was a minister in the church and my mother a deaconess. I grew up going to church at least twice a week, so from a very young age I was embedded in that church way of living. As I grew into teenage-hood, I began attending singles seminars and most corroborated what I've actually been learning all my life about marriage. I knew what divorce meant, but it was a somewhat foreign concept in that little church community where I grew up. I had one or two friends whose parents were separated, but we never talked about it openly and for the most part, there was a mother and a father in every household. I learned that marriage should be between a man and a woman, not a man and multiple women.

Homosexuality was not even talked about at all, because while it did exist and is even written in the Bible, the very idea of it was beyond most people in that conservative close-knit church where I grew up.

I learned that under no circumstances should spouses forsake each other. Even infidelity was to be forgiven. If for any reason one gets a divorce, one shouldn't re-marry either. I learned that we unmarried folks should not have sex before marriage. I have attended seminars in which the speakers opined that couples should not kiss or hug until they were both married. Some suggested that a lady should never ask a guy out, while the more open-minded ones believed it was okay. I was led to believe that choosing a life partner is the most important decision one would ever make, next to the decision of salvation. Children were encouraged at a very tender age to pray for life partners. It never occurred to anyone that we may choose a different path in life, like choose not to get married. Just like Oprah.

Marriage was a treasured institution held in the highest esteem. I was raised to cherish marriage. I especially loved the kind I imagined the pastors and ministers had, *the perfect marriage.* They were the ones who taught us these things. I wanted to be a pastor's wife because I loved how they would gather women together to teach them. I thought it would be nice to be in a position to do that. As a child, it never occurred to me that I could have a powerful ministry in marriage without being a pastor or a pastor's wife.

I grew up with all these ideas in head. I was determined to be a virgin until I got married and I was prepared to marry my soulmate. Someone whom God will reveal to me in a dream or vision. The only glitch in this perfect little plan was that God never spoke to me through dreams or visions. So, I figured I might need to rely on a prophet to tell me who my soulmate was.

Years later, when I had my first boyfriend at the age of twenty-three, the prophet said there **was** a fifty percent chance he may be the one and a fifty percent chance that he may not. Thanks a lot prophet, that was a lot of help!

Although, there were a number of boys around during teenage-hood, I did not date. I knew having a boyfriend increased my chances of having sex before marriage and I was so determined not to. I had male friends, but our relationships were of the platonic nature. I had my first kiss at twenty-three.

For someone who grew up as I did, moving to America at the age of sixteen was quite a challenging experience. Everything I have learned seemed almost alien even amongst so-called Christians in America. But I still held on to some of my beliefs.

We are all a product of our environment. Since living in America, I have become more open-minded on some issues. For example, I think women can ask men out. But I would not. I have way too much female pride. However, I do know of women who made the first move and who are now married.

Treating relationships as a trial and error process has never been my style. One of the reasons why I did not date in my teenage years was because I wanted to be completely sure that I was with the right person and that the relationship was headed towards marriage. Otherwise, it made no sense to me to be in a romantic relationship. To me, dating and marriage are birds of a feather. The purpose of a romantic relationship is marriage. If it's not marriage, then what is it?

In spite of my attempt to eliminate errors from my marital life, I still had pitfalls. Because how can you ever fully know a person's intention unless God chooses to reveal a person's heart to you? When I decided to have my first real romantic relationship, I chose the wrong guy.

He was a good person, but oh so wrong for me. In hindsight, I should have known it was not going to work, but my judgement was clouded by a number of factors. Namely, peer pressure, parental pressure, and the fact that he was *cute*.

Cuteness is no longer a qualification that I seek. Before considering a person as a potential date, there are some certain must have. If you do not set your standards **others** will set it for you, and you may end up not liking what they offer you. It is important to have standards. However, those standards should not be superficial.

When my first boyfriend approached me, I had finished college, I had a career, and I was pursuing my masters. Getting a husband seemed like the next logical accomplishment. Even if I wasn't going to get married immediately, I was old enough to start working towards it. This was the general consensus of everyone close me, and I felt quite pressured. Besides, it was always referenced how there were many women in their thirties desperately looking for a husband and how I should avoid ending up like them. So, when Mister Cute showed up, it made a lot of sense to go out with him. Also, I had no other viable offers at the time. Of course, I prayed like I was taught to, I told my parents about it, and the prophet said 50/50. He was young, and also pursuing his career. We were two young driven individuals who fancied each other. It seemed like a decent match.

The relationship ended seven months later. It was doomed to fail almost from the beginning. Remember I mentioned earlier that it is important to set standards? That became very important as the relationship progressed. My religious upbringing had lured me into believing what mattered most was that we were both believers. While this of course mattered, I realized there were other factors that needed to be prioritized just as much. I'd like to state that this book is not solely for believers, regardless of your religious preference, I strongly believe you can learn a lot from this book. I cannot dictate to anyone what religion they should or shouldn't marry into, but as a Christian woman, it is important that I marry a fellow Christian, so that my values which are mainly biblically based can align with that of my spouse.

However, my ex and I, in spite of being both Christians, did not see eye to eye on issues that really mattered. I believe he could have been a great guy with some other woman who held dear the very values he did and who saw life the way he did, but I was not that woman. And so, we argued regularly, and we never seemed able to communicate. I became the most difficult woman he's ever encountered, whereas most people, my family included knew me to be a simple and easy-going person. He saw a personality that I didn't know existed, but to him, it was very true and real.

To cut the long story short, I knew deep down that the relationship had little chances of surviving, but I kept at it hoping something will change. I don't accept defeat easily.

Taurus's are known to be very tenacious. But in the quest to make this relationship work I began to slowly lose a vital aspect of my identity. I was becoming compliant, all the while questioning if there was more to a relationship than what I had. And at the same time fearing that was all there was. I feared that the kind of love I imagined just did not exist.

It took me seven months to finally decide I deserved better than what I was getting. I just had to trust God that at the right time, even if I was already in my thirties, someone worthy of all I had to offer will come along. I decided I'd rather remain single than settle for a mediocre marriage. I did not want an above average relationship; I wanted an excellent **one**.

CHAPTER 3: LESSONS LEARNED

So, what's the takeaway from my personal experience with the wrong person? This experience taught me several things, including the fact that with all my education and smartness, I was not immune to making critical mistakes. I was just as liable to falling for the wrong guy as any other woman. We have probably seen instances whereby we don't understand *what a girl like that is doing with a guy like that*, and we believe she could do so much better. Well, I became that girl. But no one ever told me I could do better than that. That was something I had to tell myself. I had enough self-esteem to look at the relationship and say, if this is all there is to it, then I don't want it. I can do bad all by myself.

Unfortunately, many women stay in a relationship where they are better off being single. I have seen situations whereby a woman stays with a man who treats her like trash, takes her for granted and disrespects her. But she stays with him because she believes it is better than being single.

It's so sad to see men and women put up with an abusive relationship because they have a low self-esteem. Don't become a punching bag for anybody. Physically or emotionally do not let anyone abuse you. You are too precious, too valuable for that.

What's up with this stigmatization of singleness anyways? I am a woman who is passionate about marriage, but I will never trade my singleness for marriage if it does not deliver on all it promised.

Society needs to stop stigmatizing singleness. Many people are jumping into marriages with the wrong person just because they have been led to believe that **being** single is not okay. I propose to you that marriage is not for everyone. There are many people who are better off being single. I do not profess this to belittle marriage. Marriage is important, and do serve a number of purposes, including sex, childbirth, and companionship. But none of these reasons are worth ending up unhappy and miserable. Your happiness is primary.

There is a deep emotional connection we could share with another human being that tops sex. There are many children in the world already who need parents, childbirth should not be the major motivation for marriage. Some kids those children will turn out to be if their parents are constantly bickering at each other. While companionship is a good reason for marriage, there are people who are in relationships but are still lonely. It is the worst kind of fate, to feel lonely when you are not alone.

Besides, marriage is a giving affair, it's best to enter into it with the mindset of what am I going give rather than what am I going to receive. We may end up being grossly disappointed if we place all the expectations of fulfilling our emotional needs on another person. They are only human after all.

You've Got to Love You

This idea of self-esteem is really important. Many single people sell themselves short and settle for less than they truly deserve in marriage because they do not have a healthy self-concept. The truth is we don't need nobody to make us feel good about ourselves or make us feel worthy or deserving of love. You can love you all by yourself!

As a matter of fact, self-love is a prerequisite for a good marriage. It is highly important that you love yourself because you cannot give what you don't have. Self-love is crucial also because if you truly love yourself, you will not settle for less. You'll treat yourself better and find somebody who treats you just as good.

When the time do come to get married, there should be no doubt in your heart that this is the best out there for you. If there is any doubt that someone out there can love you better than the person you are with, vice versa, please don't get married.

There are a number of key points from my failed relationship that I need to elaborate on. Partners can have different personalities and taste. It makes for a more dynamic relationship. However, there are some must-have similarities.

In my first relationship, there were major differences in how we viewed important issues. We argued a lot and could never seem to find a way to communicate effectively. I felt like I was settling for less and always questioned if there was more to a relationship than what we had. I believe these points I'm about to discuss are a common phenomenon in many relationships.

Singles need to pay close attention to this. There is not much that can be done about this if you are married. However, if after marriage you realize that your values do not align, this may be a good time to have some serious conversation and perhaps seek counsel.

Irreconcilable Differences

Irreconcilable differences have become a major reason why couples divorce these days. Therefore, there is a need to examine this closely. What are the leading causes of the differences? On what issues do both spouses disagree? It could be as simple as gender roles, how you both relate with extended families, or how finances should be handled. Okay, those are not necessarily simple and could lead to major conflicts as I have witnessed in some relationships. Seemingly simple matters can become complicated if both parties have different and strong opinions about them, and if neither is willing to compromise.

Besides, there are some values you cannot compromise on because they define you as a person. Let's take finances as an example, one spouse may insist on a joint account for the sake of transparency and accountability, While the other may flat out refuse because he or she does not see the need for that level of transparency. A joint account may work for some couple, but it does not for most. Money matters and should not be taken with levity. It does have the ability to destroy a marriage.

This is an important conversation amongst others to have before marriage. This is why I strongly advocate that singles learn as much as they could about marriage before taking the plunge.

Pressure

Women in particular encounter an inordinate amount of pressure when it comes to marriage. Societal, parental, peer pressure, and of course the infamous biological clock.

Peer pressure comes in the form of "all my mates are getting married." This may differ from culture to culture, but in my culture, it is a big deal. If one of your friends is getting married, the focus shifts to you. Some people will go as far as asking you when is it going to be your turn? Regardless of whether or not you have a boyfriend. This could put a woman in a state of frenzy whereby all she thinks about is getting married.

Parental pressure could come from parents, family or those who are not related to her but feel entitled to her because they have known her for a long time. Women experience pressure from these people in many forms. Most of the conversations they have with her is centered on marriage. Sometimes, they make indirect comments that all boil down to marriage. Parents talk about having grandchildren, and some folks try to match make her.

It's particularly interesting how most African parents encourage their female children to focus solely on education, and then expect them to bring a man home as soon as they are done with college.

For the most part, these parents/family/close non-relatives do what they do out of concern. Seeing that the **modern** world allows for freedom of choice, they try their best to guide us towards what they believe is the right path, which can be summarized into three phases, get an education, get a job and get married. Although, their interference could be downright annoying and intrusive, they mostly interfere out of love.

But we need to learn how to tell people to mind their business if need be, because choosing a wrong life partner due to pressure is one of the worst decisions you'll ever make and can lead to fatalistic consequences.

Again, and again, I've seen women give in to pressure only to end up with the wrong mate. Yes, she got married like they wanted her to, but to the wrong husband. Unfortunately, when things start to go south, she gets most of, if not all of the blame and she's left to deal with the consequences alone. You do not want to end up like her.

Make Hay While the Sun Shines

Because the pressure to get married increases when a woman reaches a certain age (let's say 30), the best way to counter this is to make hay while the sunshine. This common saying reminds us to be cognizant of time. Sometimes are better suited for certain accomplishments than others and it's impossible to gain back lost time. We should endeavor not to miss the timing and seasons of our lives in which we are supposed to accomplish certain goals. It's like seeing a 30-year-old man in high school with teenagers. While we may find this somewhat inspiring, it also paints a comical picture. It is simply obvious that he missed his timing.

I understand we all mature at a different pace. The truth is some of us are just not ready for marriage until much later. Also, there are different circumstances as well that could hinder marrying at a younger age. It could be that we haven't met the right person, could be that someone jilted us or disappointed us or broke our heart, it could be lack of finances or a number of other different circumstances. But in many cases, women tend to focus on their education and career while leaving the area of marriage unattended until much later. So, we end up having less chances as time progresses to really focus on getting married.

However, women are great multi-taskers, nothing stops us from giving time and attention to the issue of finding a life partner while we are pursuing other goals. The earlier we start, the better, and the less we feel pressured by the society or our biological clock.

While some believe it's not in a woman's place to do the finding. I believe she still has to put herself in the position to be *found*.

Wives and mothers hold down the house and at the same time kick butts at their workplaces and they are great achievers in their careers. So, there are no reasons why young single women cannot pursue education/career and at the same time focus on this crucial aspect of life. It is never too early to start preparing for something so important. Your preparations can start with prayers or reading books such as this one.

I haven't mentioned so far, the pressure men face when it comes to marriage, but surely men do encounter pressures as well. Being that they are expected to be the provider and breadwinner of the family, a good man tries to get everything together before bringing a woman into his life. He wants to be able to at least provide for her basic needs and that of the children. But the society we live in makes it sometimes difficult to feed a mouth, not to talk of two or more. Men as a result tend to generally get married much later than women. They need the time to gather much needed resources. Also, females tend to mature faster than males. Often, we may see situations whereby the females are the ones to get married first in a family, even though their male siblings may be older. Men are definitely not exempted from societal pressure. However, women tend to face it more.

Values Must Align

Values must align. This point is so important it needs to be stressed over and over again. Values are defined as "a person's principles or standards of behavior; one's judgment of what is important in life." Other words for values include principles, ethics, morals and standards. Our values determine our every action and how we choose to conduct our lives. We may not think about it because some of them have become part and parcel of us, we do them automatically, like we would brush our teeth and take our baths in the morning. These principles have become ingrained in us that they pretty much define us as a person. They have become second nature to us.

Humans are generally expected to have some moral codes of conducts laid down by the society in which we find ourselves. These are referred to as social norms or societal mores. Some behaviors are generally frowned upon, some may land one in jail, while others are praised and encouraged. We defile some of these moral codes of conducts when we know we can get away with it, and some we uphold even when nobody is watching. But there are some basics mores we expect other people to know and uphold. It could be as simple as saying please and thank you.

In addition to societal norms, we all have individual norms that are comprised of our culture, religion, race, background, socioeconomics, and national identity. An American for example has a national identity different from that of a Chinese, Nigerian, Russian or any other country's citizen, even though America is considered a melting pot of different diverse cultures.

Different factors influence and shape the way we view life. Each individual has some certain values they hold dear just simply based on the fact that each of us are unique and there's no one in the entire world that shares our finger print. I once learned from a seminar that people should keep in mind when getting married that they are marrying at least three to four cultures. All these contribute to what a person considers important.

Firstly, there's the culture of the society at large; this refers to the societal norms mentioned earlier. For example, in Nigeria, we believe that adult children are responsible for taking care of their parents in their old age. This is a vastly different from the American culture in which the care of the elderly is left in the hands of strangers in nursing homes.

Secondly, there's the culture of the clan or tribe. In Nigeria we have something called ethnic groups, the equivalent of this in America would be the communities, for example, there is a black community, an Asian community, a Latino community and so on and so forth. These all have their individual set of norms and what is considered appropriate. If someone from a black community was marrying someone from a black community, there's already a common ground. Based on this, we would generally expect that they understand each other better than they would if marrying an outsider, and that there will be less conflict in the relationship. Although, this may not prove to be true in every case, more often than not, it is so.

In Nigeria there are three major ethnic groups and over 200 minor groups, each has their own unique nuances and intricacies.

The Yorubas, one of the major ethnic group, pride themselves on being more respectful than others within the Nigerian society. There are certain ways in which an older person must be addressed, and certain honorifics must be used to address people based on their age, gender, status and so on. Failure to adhere to this is highly frowned upon and shunned. Even when Yorubas are marrying from a different culture, their spouses are expected to adhere to these conducts as well. For example, a woman has to go on bended knees to greet her in-laws, and a man has to prostrate.

Thirdly, there's the culture of the family your spouse belongs to; this is whatever the family or parents' values. In some families for instance, education is highly valued. Most of the children are professionals and highly skilled workers and it has been so for many generations. You will hear such expressions as, "my great-grandfather was a doctor, my grandfather was a doctor, my father is a doctor, I am a doctor and my child will be a doctor." Someone who is more open-minded about the sort of career they want their children to pursue, may have a hard time marrying into this sort of family. Take for instance if the couple end up having just one child who is passionate about basketball. Some would rather their child become a basketball player instead of a doctor. They make more money, they are very famous, and they don't spend as much time in school. But the point is every family has its own culture. So, it is vital to keep that in mind when making the decision to get married.

Then there's an individual culture that a person adheres to; this may be a combination of all I've mentioned in addition to individual experiences, education, preferences, exposure and so on. For example, two women born and raised in the same household to the same parents may have a totally different mindset about how many children they want to have or if they even want any. One may want a big family while the other may be contented with just a child.

A person is coming into a marriage with all these different factors and so is the spouse. There will be more challenges marrying all these together if there are no common grounds. This is what I mean by your values aligning.

Let's say for instance, a young man who values education, and wants to pursue a PhD degree, "falls in love" with a woman who is happy with just being a high school graduate and is fine with her children being the same. Clearly, their values do not align, and the relationship may have serious issues. I am not saying couples have to see eye to eye on every single matter, that would be incredibly boring. But there are some issues that are so important they just need to merge. There must be a way to integrate all these different cultures and lifestyles. In the process of doing this, conflicts may arise. How often they do and how they are resolved, says a lot about the relationship.

Conflicts

Conflict is a normal phenomenon in every healthy relationship. They exist to guide us on what needs to be changed, fixed or improved. Conflicts are how we know where we each stand on different issues as couples. Without conflicts, we'll live under the assumptions that our relationships are without faults. But this is a false sense of security as there are no perfect humans, thereby no perfect relationships. If a relationship has not been tested through conflict, it's not authentic. However, if couples always have disagreements and find it difficult to communicate and resolve issues, then they may need to take a step back and reevaluate the relationship. It could be that they are more different than similar and have less in common than they think.

If both have strong personalities that keep clashing because they both want to go in the opposite direction rather than in the same direction, their values and belief system do not align. It could boil down to what each thinks about spending time together alone versus spending time with other people. One spouse for instance may love clubbing while the other is not about that life. This will result in conflict if one insists on going to clubs with or without the other person. Or, it could be about what the other person thinks of President Trump or his/her political leanings. Conflict and disagreements may be good indicators that they are trying to blend elements that just can't integrate, like water and oil.

Irreconcilable differences may sound like an excuse for a divorce, but it is real. The only issue is; people are supposed to figure this out before they get married not after. A relationship has a better chance of success if some basics commonalities are in place.

While people can change, there are some personality traits that never change, because they make up who a person is at his/her very core. People don't become a different person overnight. They only metamorphose into a clearer version of who they have always been. So, when people "change," it's either they were pretending to be what they are not, or they have always been the same way, but we are just seeing it clearly now, or it could be that they have matured into a fuller version of themselves.

I once learned in a lecture that we never fully know people until we have seen them in different seasons. Are they cold with the winter and hot with the summer? Of course, I am not referring to the weather patterns, but they serve as a good analogy. I am referring to circumstances of life. How will our partners respond to different circumstances that life may throw their way? How will they behave when they are broke versus when they have money? Will they be patient if a situation is taking longer to resolve? Will they exude confidence in the face of adversity? Will they exhibit faith when there is no physical evidence of what they seek? Does their character change with these different conditions?

These are some of the factors we have to keep in mind when taking that step towards marriage.

CHAPTER 4: DO NOT SETTLE FOR LESS

Marriage is like a gamble you have to take a leap of faith because there are no guarantees. We do not know the future! There is a saying in the Yoruba language, *"Oja Okunkun ni Igbeyawo."* It means, "marriage is a dark market." it's like trying to shop in the dark, you don't know what you might end up with. I once did a **pod-cast** on this topic and also discussed it in a vlog. It resonated with a number of people.

The truth is, we do not know what we are in for until we are actually in it. That is the way life is in general; we don't know what the future holds, however we wish and pray for the best. We also plan in hopes that life will go according to the plans we make. For instance, we get an education, in hopes that we will be able to secure a good job. People with bachelor's degree have better chances of securing high paying jobs than those with only a high school diploma. So, working hard to get a higher degree is now seen as an investment for the future. Some folks take out student loans, spend thousands of dollars, because they believe the risk of being stuck with debts is worth the future gains if it all works out. Unfortunately, it doesn't always work.

Marriage mirrors this truth of life. It's a risky investment we make in hopes that we will live happy and fulfilling lives. It's a total gamble that may or may not pay off. But if we must take a chance, then let's take a chance on someone who at least have some basic and vital qualities. Someone who in a manner of speaking is worth the risk and investment. Which is why we must not settle for less!

Now I'm not referring to all those superficial requirements (height, physique, looks). No, I am talking about the intangibles, those things that cannot be touched or seen. Let that person be someone who treats you like you are all that and a bag of chips. Someone who does not take you for granted, who prioritizes you, who respects and values your opinion, who loves you like mad, who cares for you, who is watching out for your future, who can help you achieve your purpose in life, who pushes you to be the best you can be, who brings out the best in you and who sees you as equal.

Too often for comfort, people settle for less than they deserve and end up managing their relationship when instead the union between a man and a woman should be a place of the greatest of joy and highest of fulfillment here on earth. It's the one place where we are supposed to be completely naked and not feel ashamed. Not just taking our clothes off, but also the veil with which we shroud our innermost being. This is the place of complete openness where you allow the other person to see into your soul and you into theirs as well. No secrets, no fear, 100 percent safe space.

We are supposed to know our spouse in the most intimate way possible, vice versa, and not just sexually. Our connection and communication are supposed to be almost telepathic to those observing because we are one with this person. Have you ever heard people say things like, "he completes my sentences" or "she knows what I'm thinking?" That's exactly what I'm talking about!

Of course, we shouldn't expect this level of intimacy to blossom overnight, but for it to have a chance to grow, some basic factors must first come together. I once mentioned in a vlog that we know when someone is the one. Not that I believe in the concept of there being only "one" person in the universe who is designated *the one*. I believe we can make marriage work with a number of different persons if we so choose and given that some certain elements fall into place. What I mean by knowing when someone is the one, is that we know when we have made a compatible match and the butterflies are also there to bear us witness.

Unless you choose to "dull yourself" as Nigerians will say, you can tell when you've made a good match. The expression is the idea that one ought to be smart about certain things. Some issues more than others require a higher level of intelligence. I consider relationships to be one of those issues because it so very critical, it can make or break a person.

We are all products of relationships, whether our parents were deeply in love with each other and came together to produce us or not. Some form of interaction took place, or we wouldn't exist. Relationships affects all of our lives; they are so important. But before I go off track, let me focus back on what I am trying to express about knowing when someone is the one. I said in my vlog that there is first of all a physical chemistry. You have to be attracted to that person or it wouldn't work. It's great to have a good character and wonderful qualities, but who are we kidding? We don't kiss people's character or hug their good behavior. The first encounter we have with people in most cases has to do with our senses. Often with what we see, but in some cases what we hear. It could be the person's voice that pulled us in. But there's always something that draws us. That physical pull has to be there.

A person can have all these great qualities, but if you're not attracted to the person, that's where it ends.

The problem however is that many of us stop at the physical level. We only check the box for physical and sexual chemistry (and for women financial stability), while we ignore all these other more important factors. Remember I mentioned earlier that cuteness is no longer a requirement on my list? Well, that's because I discovered there are more important qualities than cuteness. The physical chemistry can be off the hooks, you may want to jump on each other every time you meet, but that doesn't mean you're meant for each other. People may be good together in pictures and good together in bed, but that doesn't necessarily translate into being good together in marriage - that lifelong partnership.

There are other layers we must look into. I mentioned in one of my videos that couples have to connect on an emotional, intellectual and a spiritual level. None of these must be missing. "He just doesn't understand me," or "she just doesn't get where I'm coming from" are phrases we've heard before or something similar. It's because one or all of these factors are missing. We will never reach the highest peak of **fulfillment** in marriage that we are meant to if one of these levels of connections is missing. We will always feel that void. Sometimes, we feel it when we are in a relationship that isn't meant to be. We cannot place our finger on it because everything seems picture perfect, but something is still missing, and we know it intuitively.

I've seen this scenario play out in movies a lot, whereby a couple are about to get married but one or both of them have this foreboding that they can't shake off. They try to rationalize it because on the **surface** they both make up the perfect couple; educated, have great jobs, a great apartment, they look cute together, and they *love* each other. But something is still missing. And just before the wedding one of them calls the other and they have this heart to heart where they both agree that it's best they don't get married because they know they are about to make the biggest mistake of their lives. If only people in real life are as honest with themselves! We would save ourselves the failure of a broken marriage and the heartache of divorce.

There should be no question in your heart as to if someone is the one you're supposed to spend the rest of your life with. Your doubts and hesitations are indications, red flags that something is not quite right, and you should pay attention to them. I am not referring to pre-marital jitters, those come and go. I'm referring to that nagging feeling we keep pushing down until it's too late. Trust your intuition! Even with all the craziness and confusion going on in the world, the rate at which people divorce and all of that, there's still a high level of assurance that the marriage will last if you're with the right person.

CHAPTER 5: THREE MUST-HAVE CONNECTION

There are three basics must have connections without which navigating marriage in the 21st century will become difficult. These three connections are emotional, intellectual and spiritual. I will discuss each of this, so we can get an understanding of why they are so critical to having a successful marriage.

Emotional Connection

I mentioned a lot in my write-ups that love is not a feeling, but in retrospect the correct expression should be that love is not merely a feeling. Because there is a feeling aspect of loving whereby we feel something profound and almost indescribable for someone, but love does not end there. There's more to love than just the feelings, but the feelings are extremely important. The chemical reactions, the sparks, the butterflies or whatever we choose to call it has to be there. The intensity of these emotions may be higher on some days than others. For some couples it is a sort of sustained energy throughout the relationship that goes off like a volcano every now and then. There are times we feel more in love than others and there are times we are more emotionally in tuned with our spouses than others. But usually, the sparks fly more at the beginning of a relationship than they do as the relationship progresses, generally due to the fact that there's that excitement that comes with the newness of being in love.

It's like buying a brand-new car, you want to go everywhere with it or like receiving a fancy gift box, you want to unravel it and discover its hidden treasures. But as time goes on, it's no longer a new car or gift. You still love it, but you're not as excited over it as you were. It's now yours, it's been yours for a while, so there's no need to go gaga over it anymore. And this is what happens in most relationships. But for some people the loyalty is still there, even though the newness is gone, they still treasure the gift. As time passes, they become even more attached to it. Even when the car becomes old and beat-up and is no longer the latest model, some people are still very sentimental about it. They remember their first ride in it, they remember road trips, they remember little things and they treasure the car the more. The value of it increases to them as time goes on. Whereas some people are ready to discard the car and be done with it the moment it is no longer the latest. Relationships are the same exact way!

The question is, is yours the sort that gets better with time? Will your emotional connection outlive the next best thing you think the world has to offer? Will you grow closer or farther as time progresses? Are the feelings just a passing phase? What will sustain those emotions? I certainly hope it's not physical beauty because God forbid an accident occurs that maims the person, then what happens? What happens if the belly begins to bulge, and the head begins to go bald or the figure 8 starts turning into something else? My point is, sooner or later, those attributes will take a biological and natural cause. Will your love for this person fade with these? And I pray your love is not tied to money and other material things because even if you so happen to have all the money in the world, there will come a time when you will feel miserable and in need of one thing money cannot buy, *true love*. Did you notice that some of the most recent high-profile suicides happened because of relationship issues? These were people who had money, influence and affluence, but they lacked what money could not buy, happiness.

If the foundation of our love is based on a material condition, the love will fail when that condition is no longer there. We often shy away when asked the reason why we love our spouse, because it is generally believed that if there is a reason behind it, then it's not true love. But I propose that if there is no reason behind it, then it's nameless, I would not even attach a name to it not to talk of true love. We all know nothing exists without a purpose, then how come we expect love to be any different? Love by its nature must attach itself to an object because it is an expression, a verb, an action word. It would be counterproductive to do something without a reason. God who epitomizes love, loves us for a reason. He did not just send Christ to the world to die for no reason. He did it because He loves us. Why does God love us? He loves us because we are created in His image. When He looks at us humans, He sees Himself in us and that's why He loves us like crazy. Be honest with yourself, why do you love your spouse? It's okay to have a reason. What's not okay is for the reason to be materialistic, selfish and vain.

Intellectual Compatibility

In addition to the "feelings", you also want your relationship to be meaningful and satisfying. This entails that you connect intellectually, romantically, socially, behaviorally, financially, economically (this is not the same as financially, it's actually broader; goals, support, etc.). There is something referred to as

Emotional Intelligence (IE) which is the backbone of all you'll ever achieve as a person. If there is low EI then there is no capacity and therefore nothing to fill and therefore suboptimal output. I used the word "suboptimal" because while some are born with enviable EI, most are learned (acquired). So, connecting in the ways mentioned requires intelligence on the part of both spouses. I once wrote these exact words in a blog post. It is what makes the relationship interesting, the ability to communicate on a deeper level, converse about everything (individual interests and pursuits, art, music, career, goals, politics, etc.), challenge each other mentally, learn from each other and to contribute to each other's personal growth.

I love the movie *Coming to America*; it's one of those classics that one never gets tired of. Every single time I watch the movie, these words **grabs** my attention. Eddie Murphy's character said, "I want a woman **that's going to** arouse my intellect as well as my loins." That's what I'm talking about!

You want a partner who stirs up your intellect as well. You will have a more fulfilled and inspired relationship if you **both** connect intellectually. A similar scenario played out with Obinze's and Kosi's character in the novel *Americanah* by Chimamanda Adichie. They were a married couple who were not intellectually compatible. This ultimately led to the failure of the marriage.

Spiritual Connection

This is so very important. Many of us enter into relationships relying on our own instinct and understanding. We make decisions based on our senses and what we hope and imagine the future would be like. In many cases this works just fine. But marriage is a different ball game altogether because it involves you and another person and the only way for things to go your way is for your vision and purpose to align with that of the other person. Because God created you and your purpose, He has to be involved in your decision making, so you don't end up with someone who will derail you from your course.

When two people get married, they become partners and are both required to work and walk together, which is why the bible says two becomes one. And while you alone will chase a thousand, together you will chase ten thousand. Now that is very profound. But in a situation whereby you are not chasing the same goals, you may never fulfill purpose because you can only do so much as a unit, one individual. What I'm trying to convey is that there is a spiritual aspect to marriage because we humans are spirit beings, therefore marriage is a joining of two spirits.

Too often, people are joined together with folks who are not of like-minded spirit as they. This is so important. Some spouses will lead their partner to hell. We already see it unveiling here on earth. We have seen how one spouse derails the other and how marriage is a hellish experience for some people. A person can be good, doing great and all of that, until he/she gets together with this other folk, and we begin to wonder what happened. It's simple, they got involved with the wrong person.

Generally, evil has a stronger influence than good. So, if we enter into a relationship with someone hoping we would be able to change them, we may end up becoming the one who got changed. Because there's a spiritual world outside the physical realm of what we can see, touch, taste, smell, and hear, it is important to involve God in our decision making.

Sometimes, spouses outgrow each other. A person may fit you for the now, but they may be unfit for your future. It possible that there is a higher level in life that you are going to that they cannot come with you because they are small minded or faithless. When you marry the wrong person, your choices are you either leave them behind or you remain there at their level. I have seen a number of commentaries on social media about how it takes a woman like Michelle Obama to make a president out of a man, and young unmarried men are encouraged to marry a woman who can take them to that level.

Now some may say, there are non-believers out there who have great marriages. That is absolutely true. Life is based on principles, and all these principles were laid down by God. Humans modify or present them to make it sound like something they came up with, but if we search the scriptures, we'll find all of life's principles there. So, while some couples may not necessarily believe in God, they are applying Godly principles to their marriage and that's why it works.

The sad truth is that most Christians with all their head knowledge of God still fail to apply these principles to their lives. It is a shame indeed that 50 percent of divorced couples are Christians when the bible clearly states that God hates divorce. It is so crucial that Jesus Himself said it. We must really have a good excuse for this debacle that marriages have become in Christendom.

CHAPTER 6: IS THERE A PERFECT MARRIAGE?

So, let's say we have a picture-perfect scenario where every one of these factors works together, values align, and couples connect in all the different levels, they should be expected to have the perfect marriage right? The answer is no. There's no such thing as a perfect marriage. However, one can have a great and fulfilling marriage. But not without some work. In many cases, people expect things to all work out beautifully in their marriage because they "love" each other, but it doesn't quite work that way. Of course, it helps to a large extent if we have all of these mentioned factors covered, we already have a higher chance at success than most. But we still have to work at making our marriage what we want it to be. As late Dr. Myles Munroe said, there is a difference between having a set of tools and making the tools work for us. We may have the skills to make a marriage successful but never put them to use.

Marriage requires work and that is what many people fail to realize. Couples have to work out many issues together. Even if they got married without these basic qualities in place, they still have a shot at getting it right. But they will have to put in a lot more effort than if they have these factors in place. Either way, work is involved.

This is why I mentioned earlier that this book is for everyone, whether or not you're married. Singles can watch out for pitfalls not to fall into, while married folks can start checking the box for these elements. There may still be a chance to get it right with your partner. Divorce is not always the final option; couples can both work together to turn things around. For those who believe they've got it together, there are still one or two points you can learn to make your relationship even stronger.

Work Work Work Work Work Work

Work is defined as an "activity involving mental or physical effort done in order to achieve a purpose or result." Whatever you desire to achieve in your marriage, whatever the purpose is, whether to have amazing lives together, raise wonderful children, fulfil God's purpose, have unrestricted sex, love each other forever, or whatever it may be, you each need to put in the effort to achieve it. This is the price tag for a long-lasting marriage!

The effort is not limited to mental and physical alone. In fact, depending on the area in which you wish to achieve a goal, the kind of effort becomes different. If the goals are multiplex, then you need to put in work in multiple areas. For example, if you want a better sex life, you have to put in the effort to achieve that; exercise, read books, learn, and communicate preferences with your partner. If you want to communicate better, you cannot just keep to yourself or argue all the time or spend hours on social media. You have to find effective ways to communicate. You may need to read some books, attend some counseling sections, or do some research. Let's say the goal is for one spouse to achieve a certain feat, maybe lose weight, finish school, or learn something new, both partners have to work to achieve that goal together. You may both need to gym together. The other spouse may need to put in extra time and effort around the house in order for the spouse who needs to accomplish the goal to be able to do so. You cannot be lazy in your marriage! That's the place you're supposed to be the most productive.

I know for most people work is an unpleasant word because we think of the process rather than the satisfying end result. But work is not always unpleasant, it can be enjoyable, especially if you're doing it for a good cause or with great people. In this case for the sake of your relationship with the love of your life, to make your marriage all you desire for it to be. Marriage is a joint effort; it is important for both partners to do things together to achieve their goals. These reverts back to all I've mentioned thus far, couples need to be compatible in many ways, and their values must align.

I always stress that a relationship is as good as the two units involved. It does not depend on one partner being all of that and doing all of that while the other person just rides along with very little to contribute. Couples are supposed to complement each other. In the area the other person is lacking, you're able to fill the gap, vice versa. Just like the male and female body fit together and complement each other. It doesn't make for a pretty picture or a good marriage when both spouses are lacking in the same essential areas.

CHAPTER 7: WHAT WE LEARNED IN BIOLOGY CLASS

There's something referred to as codependency, independence and interdependence. The best way to illustrate this is through biology. There's something taught in biology classes called symbiosis. Symbiosis in a simplified term is the living together of biological organisms in which there are three different kinds of relationships, mutualistic, commensalism, or parasitic. There are some organisms that can live independently of each other but choose to live together and depend on each other.

In the best-case scenario this is what marriage should be. This is what is referred to as interdependency. A man and a woman come together to rely on each other, even though they can choose to live life individually and still be productive, happy, and wealthy.

But these two individuals figured no one is an island, there are some goals they can accomplish better and faster with someone walking through life with them. Also, a warm body to cuddle up to every now and then is really nice. Plus, there is a need for sexual release and emotional interaction, and the best way to get that is through marriage.

Mutualistic Symbiotic Relationship

A mutualistic symbiotic relationship can be by choice or necessity. In some human relationships, you need the other person. Some people can go through life without marriage; they may choose to marry if they so please. But for others, it's a need. There are certain accomplishments that can only be achieved through marriage. A great example of this would be the story of Adam and Eve. Adam had the seed of all humanity in him but for him to release it to produce humans, he needed Eve.

Marriage is also the final destination of romantic love. It's the highest demonstration of romantic love. It's in marriage that we truly get to show the world and the other person that we know how to love.

Human wants are insatiable. It's not realistic to put the burden of fulfilling all our wants and needs on another human. No one but you is responsible for your own happiness. However, a certain level of dependency is expected in marriage. While marriage can be facultative for those who choose to get married, I believe it's best if there is a need attached to it. If we don't see a need for the other person, we are likely to trivialize the union or take the other person for granted. A healthy level of neediness/dependency is okay. Plus, it feels good to be needed (smiles) .

Commensalistic Relationship

In a commensalism relationship, one of the partners gains but not to the detriment of the other. But human relationships are such whereby the actions of one spouse in some way whether good or bad, has an effect on the other spouse. Human relationships are more mutualistic or should be.

Parasitic Relationship

A parasitic relationship is the kind of relationship no one deserves to have, but unfortunately many find themselves in this situation. This is a relationship in which one partner gains at the detriment of the other. This is what is known as Codependency, a type of relationship where "one person supports or enables another person's drug addiction, alcoholism, gambling addiction, poor mental health, immaturity, irresponsibility, or under-achievement." Do you get the picture? Some people get married to someone who is so needy that he or she ends up draining the partner, in some cases emotionally, in some cases financially, in some cases mentally and so on and so forth. Because one partner does not have it together, the other has to overcompensate for what is lacking in that person's life. The relationship becomes a choking prison rather than a place of freedom and joy.

For a while, it may be okay providing so much support to a grown individual who should be able to stand on his or her own feet, but after a while, it gets frustrating and it takes a toll on the relationship. All things remaining equal, no one should have to deal with a partner who is a burden and liability to them. I understand life happens and people sometimes get into unfortunate situations and may need that shoulder to lean on. One spouse could lose his or her job and need to depend on the other spouse, they may fall sick or have an accident that requires that they be supported or may be going through a grieving experience and just need the other person to be there. But no one should have to constantly deal with a spouse's immaturity, lack of motivation and drive, addiction, and **under-achievement**. It wears down the relationship.

Individuals who desire to enter into a committed relationship should first of all get their acts together. A relationship should not be a place where people come to hide away from being all they can be because they are too lazy to go for their dreams and goals. A relationship is a place where two people push, encourage, inspire and motivate each other to be the best version of themselves. It is key that you never stop developing yourself, never stop cultivating yourself, and never stop evolving. Even when you're gray and old and have spent all these years living together with your partner, you still have to keep pushing and striving to be an even better version of you. A relationship is as good as the two individuals involved.

If both individuals are great human being of high quality, the relationship has a much better chance at success.

Becoming Whole

How do you become an excellent individual? By continuing to improve on yourself. Learn new things, explore, go for it, plan, strategize, work hard, give it your all, serve God, serve humanity, be good, be fit, and love like it's your purpose!

This is so very important. To be self-sufficient is perhaps the greatest accomplishment an individual could have. To be able to stand on your own, think for yourself, have a relationship with God, and be a whole individual (financially stable, mentally, spiritually, and emotionally sound)   .

God who is the Creator of this institution called marriage gave a formula that we tend to always miscalculate.

The scriptures states, "two shall become one." Meaning, one complete individual plus another complete individual makes up the union called marriage. Not half and half, not one and half, but two become one. But there are too many people entering into marriage as halves. They are not self-sufficient, they are emotionally damaged or immature with no sense of direction, no definitive goal, and they are full of all sorts of baggage. The worst-case scenario is for two individuals like this to get married without first resolving their issues. How do we expect such a marriage to work?

It is just as bad when someone like this lashes on to someone who is a complete individual? The relationship becomes parasitic whereby the parasite causes damage to the host.

Dear readers, it is important for us to work on ourselves and take steps towards becoming all that God intended for us to be. Everyone was born to succeed. Although, we may get into some unfortunate circumstances in life. But as long as it is within your means to do so, always push yourself to be better. Work on yourself and direct that same energy towards your marriage. Do not be lazy.

It's the Most Important Decision *Ever*

The decision of whom to spend the rest of our lives with is a serious one. I hope I've demonstrated that thus far in this book. It is so crucial for us to be smart and wise about it. Marriage is not a place to walk into with the blindness that love supposedly has. Love is said to be blind, but I propose that the blindness is deliberate. Being in love with someone does not equal being blind to their faults or shortcomings. How can we profess to truly love someone when we don't see them in their entirety, flaws and all? It's not logical, and yet this is what we claim. If we love someone, we see them for who they are and accept them, but we also want them to be a better person. In many cases, we see that they are living beneath potential, so we strive to push them to be the best they can be.

If someone claims to love you and he or she is not pushing you towards your goals and purpose, the person is lying. If you love somebody, you'll want them to be better. You will not want the person to continue living with the same flaws, attitudes and character that are impeding their success. Some flaws are manageable, but there are some major ones that you either fix before you get married or you end the relationship altogether.

I repeat, you don't want to be married to someone hoping the person will change when he/she may never change. If you know whatever issue that person has will be a source of conflict in the marriage, please don't get married. If for example someone has been cheating on you when you were dating, he or she cheated when you got engaged; you do not need me to tell you it will happen when you get married! Ladies and gents, please use your medulla oblongata! If someone is rude to your family and friends and disrespects you, marriage isn't going to make them change. A high maintenance lady will continue to be so; her taste will only grow more expensive after marriage; can you afford her lifestyle?

We need to realize that marriage only amplifies existing issues, it doesn't solve problems. If we get married hoping it will be a fix to whatever issues personal or mutual we already have, I guarantee you that it will not. If a spouse has anger issue for example, marriage is not going to soften his/her heart, if anything it will worsen the issue because of the added responsibility and pressure. Don't let your love be blind, remove that veil and see people for who they truly are!

Some people do pretend to be what they are not, which is why we need to be careful and prayerful. It's okay to do some investigations, and background checks if we must (I learned this the hard way). People reveal themselves through their words, have lots of serious conversations. No topic should be off limits. Talk about your goals and aspirations, your vision for the family, get into real conversation about childbirth, physical health plan, career progression, interests, business, academic or extracurriculars. Break the relationship into phases, talk about investment plans, talk about responsibilities towards extended family (dad, mom & siblings).

Date wisely, don't do movie dates all the time or other places where there's really no opportunity to talk. Seek counsel and read the same types of books about relationships and marriage so you're both getting the same types of information. Create a plan together towards achieving each purpose, whereby both individuals specifically commit to every plan to see the purpose achieved.

Ask deliberate questions on whether your spouse is getting enough from you, that is a way to get better at loving each other, protecting each other's interests and having a great relationship.

Above all, do not settle for less than you're worth in life or in a relationship. Make hay while the sun shines so you don't end up scrambling around when it's too late. At that point, many people end up settling for whatever they get.

Make yourself an attractive prospect to good folks who are out there searching. Trust God for the best and be realistic, not superficial.

CHAPTER 8: BE CAREFUL OF WOLVES IN SHEEP'S CLOTHING

I am a firm believer in the saying that "as you make your bed, so you must lie on it." In other words, our actions/decisions/choices have consequences. I am a believer; I am not ashamed of the gospel of Christ. But there may be folks reading this book who do not believe in Jesus, so you may not understand what I am referring to when I say I thank God for the grace of Jesus Christ and the work that the blood that was shed on the cross accomplishes in my life, because it cancels out a lot of costly errors that could otherwise have destroyed my life. There are some mistakes that we cannot recover from. They are just too costly. Some of us will notice how our parents and other older folks say things like, "I don't want you to make the same kinds of mistake I made." In many cases, it's because they are still suffering the repercussions of those mistakes.

My decision not to date prior to completing a college education was so I could abstain from sex, I was realistic enough to know there are not a lot of guys out there who will permit celibacy in a romantic relationship. And being that I am a believer, I was trying to do it God's way. I am not writing this to in any way portray myself as a person of excellent moral character. I am human, just like everyone else. I get tempted, I fall short, but I thank God for grace. I just believe it's important for me to share my story because it has the potential to bless someone, and if by virtue of my life, just one person is changed then my job is done.

I didn't date while all my mates were and there was quite a lot of peer pressure to. For crying out loud, I am a young attractive red-blooded maiden (smiling at that word), and I find the opposite sex equally attractive. Plus, I was no longer in my small community church in Nigeria where I was constantly being reminded of just how grieve the sin of extramarital sex is. I was in America where everything goes. The only thing standing between me and the lifestyle that many young folks were living was my conscience and I find throwing your conscience away is one of the easiest things to do in America. There is so **much** licentiousness. It was very important for me to protect myself and my dignity, and I took my beliefs seriously. Being saved to me was not a joke.

Do friends frown at me and make fun of me for being one of those people who doesn't party till they drop? And for being the only one who doesn't know how to contribute to conversations about sex? Yes! But I held on firmly to my beliefs, until I was out of college.

In my culture, earning a degree automatically qualifies you for a husband. As a matter of fact, you are overqualified and overdue for one. Plus, I had a good job, so what else was I waiting for? The pressure I was able to wave off when I was younger (I'm still very young), became too overwhelming and it came constantly from my parents and loved ones. Mind you, I was only twenty-two when I completed my bachelor's, but that did not make any difference to my folks. After all, my mates in Nigeria were already getting married or so they reminded me.

Being that we live in America, where many lifestyles are permissible, my parents were afraid I may end up never getting married or waiting until it was too late. So, when at twenty-three I introduced to them a guy who had asked me out, they joyfully accepted him. When they should have **instead** asked some serious questions to make sure I was making the right decision.

They were just happy to see me with a man. I am not blaming my folks; I am just pointing out their errors. At the end of the day, it was my decision to enter into a relationship with this person.

If I was a stronger individual, I wouldn't have given in to parental pressure.

I was not an outgoing person, so I knew it was very unlikely for me to meet my partner at a party (this seemed to be the case for many of my friends). Over the last couple of years, I have become more extroverted. I hoped that I will meet someone at church, but I was actually focused on meeting someone online. Yes, I wanted to meet someone online, more specifically on Facebook. I do not have the aversion that some people do to meeting folks online. I believe it could be a starting point and the relationship could transition offline from there. I had this strong conviction that I will meet someone online. I had this vision of someone coming across my profile and seeing what he likes so much so that he is compelled to take a closer look, and from there love will blossom (told you I'm a romantic). That was exactly how I pictured it happening.

So, I kept waiting and waiting for it to happen. I never went after guys myself; I figured if he doesn't come by himself, then he is not interested. Every now and then I'll get a request and engage in conversations with men, but they were mostly geographically unattractive. But I was not discouraged, I kept hoping to meet someone online. Therefore, I presented myself extremely well on Facebook. (Be careful what you wish for, you just might get it!)

When Mister Cute sent me a friend request, the first thing I noticed was that he was geographically suitable, he lived in America and more specifically in New York. I am a New Yorker, he is a New Yorker, perfect! We got into a conversation and it became obvious just how close we lived to each other, we even had close mutual friends. We chatted every single day afterwards. Mostly we said hey and hello, just seeing how you're doing, things of that nature. Interestingly, a week later, we met at a friend's engagement party. It was unplanned, I didn't know he was going to be there, he didn't know I was going to be there, but when it happened, I took it as a sign of something really good. Surely God has answered my prayer and has finally sent me someone. So, when roughly two weeks later, he asked me out, I said yes. Where there warning signs that the relationship was not going to work? Yes, plenty in fact, but I was in love.

The timing was right; it would save me from all the hassles and questioning from my parents and church folks about marriage. My parents were happy, he had friends who vouched for him and these were people whom I knew and trusted. So, what if he was rough around the edges? What if he lacks patience and gets angry at every little thing? What if uses profanity? What if he clubs? That doesn't make him a sinner, right? All those things are minor anyways; he could change with time. And so, I rationalized myself into dating him. But we were so different that we ended up getting into disagreements *constantly*. When we were not contending about something, it was because we simply weren't communicating with each other at all. This happened a lot. Sometimes we would not speak for days, *sometimes weeks*.

For the most part, we didn't have anything to talk about because we had little to no mutual interests. When we do have serious conversations however, they end in conflicts because we had completely two different mindsets about what we wanted for our lives. Being the woman, I was expected to be the one who compromises or "submits," but I could not submit to something that would not bring me joy and I could not compromise on my values. No matter how hard we tried to make it work, it just didn't fit together because it was not meant to be in the first place.

We were like oil and water, and we constantly got frustrated. We were too good folks, but just not right for each other. It got to a point I just knew I couldn't continue like that. I was not his type of woman, although I believed I had all the qualities any man would want in a woman. I tried to fit into what he wanted, but by doing that, I was losing a sense of who I was and what makes me a really unique and great individual. However, I accepted it all in good faith, thinking it was all part of the relationship process. I knew I wasn't perfect, so maybe he was right. Maybe I needed to change in certain areas. But soon I realized no amount of changes would be enough and there was nothing wrong with me to begin with! He just couldn't see me for who I am because it was beyond him. He was incapable of understanding me.

We had the hots for each other, certainly. We looked good together, we "loved' each other, but we just didn't connect on all the other levels I have analyzed. We certainly tried, but it just could not work. If one of us had not said you know what this is not working, let's call it quit, we would have ended up getting married because at least, we were compatible in the physical aspect of the relationship. But that was not enough. And time was not what we needed.

Time will make no difference. In time, we may learn to drop matters to avoid arguing about them. We may learn to live separate lives as a married couple and come together only for recreational purposes, but we will never attain that full fulfillment we ought to have. That complete joy and intimacy will never be there. There will always be something missing, because the emotional connection was lacking, the spiritual connection and the intellectual connection were not there. These were the things I realized when seven months later, I decided to end the relationship. It was a rough ordeal.

Afterwards, I questioned God because I believed I deserved better considering I have lived a pretty decent life. I shouldn't be the one to get heartbroken and end up in a relationship where the other person just does not see me for my worth. I felt cheated because having kept myself for so long; I should end up with someone who will appreciate and value me. Then I **began** to realize that the signs were there all along, but I ignored them. Sadly, many of us do that. I also realized that I didn't trust God enough not to short change me. I quickly fell into the arms of the first man who came along. I gave in to pressure, I listened to the stories of how difficult it is to find a husband and how there are many women out there who are desperate, and so I entered into a relationship that wasn't what I deserved. I settled for less.

But thank God there was enough sense and confidence in me to get out of the relationship. It got to the point where I had to say; I'd rather be single than end up having less than a fulfilling marriage.

I felt like the prodigal son who came to his senses, and said I'd rather be a servant in my father's house than eat pig's food in another man's house. I came to my senses and said I'd rather be single than get married only to be forced to divorce at the end of the day. We all have to trust God for the right person! Don't enter into a relationship with just anybody, anyhow; you're more valuable than that.

When I Ended It

Everyone thought I was crazy, "why do you want to break up

when he didn't cheat on you?" "do you have someone else already?" "why not hold on to him until someone else comes along?" "there are no good men out there" "if the good outweighs the bad just stay with him" "he's not as bad as some of the ones I've dated" "give it a second chance" ......These were some of the things that were said to me. I could have listened and let the fear of not finding another person hold me down, or the fear of finding someone worst, but I was resolute. The amount of pressure I received from folks telling me to keep the relationship was even more than when they were encouraging me to get a boyfriend. But knowing what I knew, knowing he wasn't the one for me, I just couldn't continue the relationship.

If my story sounds familiar to you, perhaps you are is in a similar relationship, I pray from the bottom of my heart for confidence to realize you are worthy of love, the real deal. And that you deserve to have a fulfilling relationship.

The moment I made the decision to end the relationship, it was as if some floodgates of heaven opened and it rained down men. I have never encountered so many eligible bachelors in my life and in such a short period of time as well. Young mature eligible men, doctors, engineers, lawyers and other professionals, single or divorced who were ready to settle down and they all came after me. I was overwhelmed, it was like a dream. I had so many options to choose from and all these men approached me on

Facebook! It was at the time when my blog was slowly taking off, and I posted a lot of content from my blog to Facebook. I guessed they were not only attracted to my beauty but my brain as well.

As a single lady, I learned an important lesson from this experience. It is not enough to be just physically appealing. You must do something with your life that adds to your value. It's great to have an education and a job, but beyond that, utilize the Internet and social media to do something positive and beneficial to the world around you. Some of us have over a thousand friends and followers. Those people represent opportunities to impact lives. You could make a career out of social media or meet some great people.

Imagine getting over 100 friend requests daily from the opposite sex who wanted to get to know you? Yes, it happened to me and I was not even a celebrity. At some point I had to turn off the friend request function on Facebook.

This time around, I **believed** that God was giving me a chance to choose and it was imperative that I choose wisely. I felt like a lady on the *Bachelorette show*; I even had more choices that the show permitted. I narrowed my choices down to ten and from there to three and from three to two. These were decisions I had to make quickly because I didn't want to lead anyone on or waste anyone's time. If I continued to wait before making a decision, I will only grow confused. Too many choices could be an enemy of decision making.

When there were so many choices, what **were** the odds of choosing the right person? I honestly don't know. Because I'm an intelligent person and a great conversationalist with an excellent sense of humor, it's usually very easy for people to connect with me. Men in particular find me easy to converse with. I have had many men tell me that it feels as if they've known me forever, just from one conversation. I knew I had that kind of effect on men. On days I feel like being silly, I refer to myself as a fame fatale (laugh).

My process of elimination was done by most of the things I've mentioned. Some of these men were not in New York, so they **traveled** down from their various states to see me. Some of them I prevented from coming. Some were willing to take their chances even though there were no guarantees. I had to rely mostly on the conversations we had to make my decision, but more so I believed God was involved in the process. Looking back on how I handled the situation with such aplomb, I must say that I am very impressed. I made a few mistakes along the way like giving false hopes or not being firm enough when I said I'm not interested or being carried away by how attractive a man **was**, but overall, I handled the situation well.

There was a part of me that loved all the attention, but there was also a part of me that knew I had to seize the opportunity. Some of those men are now my good friends, and I could easily go to them if I needed their expertise or knowledge and they'll be happy to oblige (with no strings attached).

Let me take a step back here and say not every man who sent me a friend request wanted to date me. But some of them just wanted friendship, some wanted to work with me, some just admired what I was doing, some wanted to advise me, some wanted to help me, some were just fans, and so on.

For those who wanted a romantic relationship, I narrowed it down to two and it was a tougher decision deciding between the two than it was when there were ten. I was equally attracted to both. So how did I eventually make my decision? They both presented themselves as good men, hardworking, educated, mature and ready to settle down. I believed they will each treat their wife like the sun and moon sets and rises on her. Our values aligned or, so it seemed. But mine was not the case of being in love with two men as it happens so often in *The Bachelorette*. As a matter of fact, that feeling of love was quite the farthest thing from my mind. I guess this should have been a good indication of how un-right it was.

The way I dealt with the situation was akin to how a business transaction or arranged marriage is dealt with. I had just ended a relationship with a man who I was supposedly in love with. I had all these men with better qualities coming after me and I needed to make a decision. I wish I knew then some of the things I know now. I had to pray, trust God and choose. I know it sounds very mechanical and calculated. There were none of the warm and fuzzy feelings you'd expect when someone is choosing a life partner. I have done the falling in love thing before and it did not work so I thought this time around I could do without it. I was wrong.

There was nothing clouding my judgment, I knew exactly what it was I was doing and why I chose who I chose. These were men I could afford to take chances with, they were both excellent men or, so I thought. But a couple of things that may seem minor, finally made me pitch my tent in the direction of one of them.

A Testimony in Progress

Life was good. I was walking on sunshine. There I was, this young beautiful, highly educated, smart and accomplished woman and all these men wanted me! I was on top of the world. Little did I know there was a serpent in my paradise.

He had this uncanny ability to see through me. Almost as if he had spent years studying me and knew all there was to know. This was what made him stand out more than anything else. He always said the right things, as though he knew my thoughts before I formed them. He attributed this ability to his discipline as a medical doctor. I took it for granted that he had spent a great deal of time studying psychology. I deluded myself into thinking we have an out of this world connection, something akin to a spiritual bond.

Our very first conversation lasted for hours and from that day we kept talking. When I first received his friend request on Facebook, I had several other men who were also reaching out to me. He sent a message and I ignored him. I was too overwhelmed already. I was not responding to every single person; I was not adding every single person either. But a few hours later I decided to respond, because he seemed like a responsible man and I didn't want to be rude (my niceness was my undoing). So, I said hello and from there it continued. He was highly intelligent. I have engaged in many intellectual conversations, so I was not surprised to learn he was a doctor. He stretched my brain and I found myself trying to match him every step of the way. I began using words that I would normally look up first in the dictionary. In one night, we covered politics, religion, family, career, personal style, goals, marriage, Nigeria, America, and books. I was at the point where very little impressed me because I've met so many men already, but he definitely caught my attention, and it had nothing to do with his physique.

Actually, he was not the most attractive man to approach me. My other choice was far more good looking and equally intelligent and well-spoken, and we connected as well. As the relationship progressed, I would later joke that when I met him, he looked like the black version of Humpty Dumpty. I encouraged him to lose weight and he obliged. I looked past what he looked like on the outside to what came out of his mouth which I thought was a reflection of his heart. His mental capacity more than his physique drove my decision making. How could I have known I was being hoodwinked?

If my decision was purely based on looks, I had one other potential suitor, a doctor as well, who was younger and very handsome, and he fancied himself head over heels in love with me. But my decision could not be based on looks. Considering my previous relationship, I tried not to put too much emphasis on that. I was looking for someone with whom I connected beyond the physical level, but emotionally, intellectually, spiritually, socially, behaviorally, etc. And although I found these connections in two men, I had to choose one.

I chose the one whom I thought was more ready and eager, only to discover he was a masterful player who had deliberately approached me with impure motives. You see, it was all a game to him. He wanted to prove a point to himself that he was able to get a woman like me to fall in love with him. Apparently, he had perceived me to be a magnificent woman of some sort (I was in my own right) .

He believed the only way he could gain access to me was by presenting a false version of himself. Truth be told, if he had revealed his true identity, he would never have been considered as a viable prospect. He was a lying pretentious human being and I fell for every single one of his carefully selected lies. He presented himself as everything I could ever ask for in a husband, but it was all a facade. It was like the devil presenting himself as an angel of light.

I never considered myself a naive woman. I am smart; I have my straight A's, honors and degrees to prove it. But in retrospect, I did not realize just how vulnerable I was. It never occurred to me that a man would approach me just to toy with me. I have heard all sorts of similar stories. It has happened to women I know! *All About Camila* was my favorite childhood soap opera. But the thought that it could ever happen to me just never crossed my mind. I was a bright young woman who was just starting out her life. I was looking to meet someone who was genuinely interested in me and hopefully building something great together. It never occurred to me that a person would approach me out of deceit. Whatever his reason was, it was depraved.

When after nine months of dating, I discovered he was married with two kids (information he was disinclined to give me at the onset), I castigated myself for being so stupid. My confidence and pride took a nosedive.

I was played by a professional womanizer who for reasons unfathomable targeted me as his victim. He packaged himself as someone who respected women, values their opinion, and sees them as equal. A presentation he knew I would fall for being the feminist that I am. The giveaway should have been the fact that he had spent most of his adult life in Nigeria prior to moving to America and it's not typical of African men to lean towards feminism. But I thought his level of education differentiated him. Apparently, I was wrong. He only pretended to be what he was not. If he truly respected women, he would not have preyed on my vulnerability. I suspect he had a total contempt for women, particularly his wife whom he claimed to have divorced prior to moving to America.

I would never truly know the reason why he approached me and deceived me. I have only his explanations and my summations. But on the day that I met him for the last time, after I discovered he was a liar, he begged my forgiveness and even asked for a second chance (as if). I remember telling him that I had never gone through such a momentous life experience before, but I believed God allowed it, so I could not only have a story to share, but so I could become a stronger and wiser person.

How is it that I chose the worst possible person out of hundreds of men? I who dished out advice on marriage and relationships; be smart, be wise, shine your eyes, and so on. It was a nightmare.

I was so sure of this person I introduced him to my family, shared my innermost secrets with him, my dreams, goals and desires, not knowing I was being manipulated.

So, if you have ever been through a heartbreak, I get it. I know what that feels like. Thinking of what could have been with any one of the other men, particularly the second man with whom I had also developed a friendship, I go crazy.

We've probably heard the saying, "time heals all wounds." Well, the truth is it does not. At the time we are going through our painful experiences, we may feel like the world is coming to an end or wish that it actually would. But time blunts the severity of the pain. Just like a physical wound, it's most painful when it's fresh, but afterwards the pain begins to dwindle as the wound begins to heal. We may get a scar as a reminder that we got injured, even though the physical pain is no longer there. There will always be a reminder of emotional wounds as well, and we may not completely get over it. But in time we may learn to live with it, trust ourselves, forgive the other person and forgive ourselves.

I decided not to pay more regard to this depraved individual than he is worth. So, I'll write no further about this particular blob on my otherwise relatively wonderful life. I have forgiven him. A friend once told me that by making excuses for other people, she was able to forgive them. If someone did something hurtful to her, she tries to rationalize why they would do that and, in the process, she was able to more easily forgive their shortcomings. I mention this because putting yourself in the other person's shoe may be a good method for someone out there. But personally, I cannot rationalize why he would do that and I cannot ever imagine doing that to another human being. It's just plain evil.

For women (and men) out there who have been deceived or hurt, I want to take this opportunity to empathize with you. You are not alone. It happens to the best of us. It's not your fault that you opened up your heart and gave them a chance. It's their fault for violating your trust. Stop blaming yourself for another person's shortcomings and wrongdoing. Forgive yourself for making that stupid mistake. You are only human after all; you are liable to making mistakes and falling into errors. And know this, you are worthy of love. You are worthy of being cherished. You deserve someone who will be true and faithful to you. No matter your past mistakes, you deserve a second chance. Let it go and learn to trust yourself.

I refused to be a victim, even though I was victimized. I looked at my oppressor in the eyes and told him that I will not give him that power over me. I told him that this experience will not hold me back from trusting again. I will not go into a shell or build a cocoon of distrust and suspicion around me. I refuse to think all men are liars and cheaters and heartbreakers. Not even for one moment did I allow myself to entertain that thought because I know it is not true, and no lying deceitful man will make me think any differently.

Did I become more cautious and careful? Yes, certainly! Once bitten, twice shy as the saying goes. It's okay to become more guarded. As a matter of fact, we all need to guard our hearts against people with impure motives and bad intentions. Don't fall for every Tom, Dick and Harry! But in the process of being guarded we have to be careful not to keep the good ones out.

I do have a feeling though that the right one will stick around longer than most.

CHAPTER 9: MY LOVE AND HATE RELATIONSHIP WITH AFRICAN MEN

I love African men, particularly Nigerian men. But I can't stand many of them with their archaic notions of gender roles. I want to marry a Nigerian man, but not if I can't find one who genuinely understands me. Many of the Nigerian men I've encountered so far have treated feminism with condescending tolerance. They are willing to accept the idea of gender equality as something in vogue, but when it comes to the practicality of it, particularly in a romantic relationship, they are quick asserting their masculinity. I don't understand why some men feel so threatened by the idea of women having equal rights in society.

Now as a Christian woman, I understand that the roles of each person have to be defined in a marriage, and by the order of things as God designed it, the husband is the head of the household and the wife is the helpmate. There is no need to oppressively reassert this structure.

A man being the head of the house does not automatically equal a woman being a lesser person. In single parents' household where the man is absent, we have seen women step up to do a fantastic job of leading the household. Women have leadership qualities just as men do. We are equally created by God.

The reason why nature ordered it that a man be the head is so there is no confusion. If two people are leading the same group, there's bound to be chaos. Women can lead too and do lead in the absence of a man. But the way God designed it is for the man to lead and God has placed some certain characteristic in the male that makes him fit for that role, the same way God placed some qualities in the woman that complements the man.

If Adam the first man was so sufficient and wonderful all by himself, there would have been no need for Eve. But there was a missing piece in that man's life. He needed someone who was like him, could be his companion and could support him. He had all these animals to keep his company, and he had a job taking care of the garden, but still something was missing, and so God created Eve.

Eve was a complete individual just as Adam was, but different. Our differences do not make us unequal! If we look beyond the body, we are all the same; we are all spirits and spirits have no gender (nor color). The bible even takes it further and states, "male and female, young and old, Jew or Gentile, slave or free we are all one in Christ." Meaning God sees us equally. He is not partial to us based on our gender.

But for the sake of orderliness, God arranged the family unit in such a way that the man is the head, and this mirrors the Trinity; God the Father, the Son and the Holy Spirit. All equally God, but in the order of things, God the Father is first. This mirrors Christ and the church as well. He is the head; the church is the body. The head needs the body to expend all of its capabilities, vice versa. They co-exist together.

The scriptures refer to Christ as the firstborn among many brethren who are the church, who are joint heirs. Marriage between a man and a woman should be viewed in a like manner, and because it's a love relationship, no one should feel superior or lesser. Love does not see itself as more important than the other person. It is not pompous or boastful.

If we pattern our lives according to Jesus's principles, Christ demands that the person who sees himself as the greater should serve the lesser. But all my life living in Christendom, I have mostly seen women being treated as second-class citizens, especially in their own homes and they are highly underappreciated. Many women are made to feel like being a woman is a terrible fate. Religion and culture are used as excuses to treat women as less valuable creatures of God, in comparison to men.

I by no means disregard bible verses such as Ephesians 5:22, and 1 Corinthians 14:34 that are used to justify the unequal treatment of women. But rather than the eagerness to prove that they are right, and the bible supports them, I pray that the hearts of men will be filled with love that is not self-elevating, or boastful. If our hearts are so filled with love, we would not abuse or overemphasize our position.

Fellas, you don't need to demand that she submits to you, if you're doing what you are supposed to do as a man, she will.

Sadly, some men are either very insecure or have over-inflated egos. Women do themselves more harm than good by making themselves appear subservient in order to make the man feel better about himself. A man would not need a woman to inflate his ego, if he has confidence in himself. A real man is not afraid to let his woman shine. He gives her all the support and encouragement she needs, because while she is pursuing her purpose, he is not lazing around, he is also pursuing his.

My Wish Above All

My desire is that people, both men and women will not live haphazard and mediocre lives, when in fact they can do so much more. I do not exempt myself from all these admonitions. I am striving hard as well to fulfill my destiny and live to my fullest potential. With all I have written so far in my blogs and said in my vlogs about relationships and marriage, in addition to all I have written in this book, I anticipate that certain expectations will be placed on me to have an exemplary marriage. I absolutely intend to!

I'll outline now some of the tools I believe make love last forever. What I intend to put into practice and what I believe would help and perhaps save many marriages out there. As stated earlier, every relationship is unique. One size does not necessarily fit all, but there are some general guidelines that make the path to success smoother.

Thank God I was able to find out the man I was seeing was a deceiver before it was too late. I consider myself extremely blessed. Some women are not so lucky. Some women get married to these types of men before they realize they've married a devil. I had a narrow escape.

CHAPTER 10: THE FOUR PILLARS OF MARRIAGE

Permit me to use this illustration to describe a marriage. Marriage is like a house. The foundation that makes up the building are the elements I have covered so far, physical/sexual attraction, compatibility, and alignment of values/visions/goals. I'd like to add that genetic compatibility is also critical.

Without those elements the building will collapse. Those who are familiar with architecture know that the foundation is critical to a building, it determines how tall, or large or sturdy a building can be. The height of the building and how much weight it is expected to carry, determines the depth of the foundation. If you want your life or marriage to be a tall magnificent mansion, it's better you start laying the foundation early on. If we desire for a marriage that is built to withstand any elements (it can wither the storms and hurricanes of this life), then we better start digging deep. Remember as you make your bed, so you must lie on it. As you've laid your foundation, so you must build on it.

Disaster is what happens when we are trying to add to a building whose foundation is not built for the extra weight or height. The building can collapse, leading to loss of properties, money and in many cases lives.

You determine the quality of life you want to live and the kind of marriage you want to have by investing in yourself and putting into yourself those things that increase your value and make you a better person. You cannot lay a weak foundation and expect to build a mansion on it, it is not possible.

We all want the best and finest things in life, but only a few are willing to pay the sacrifice for them. We are impressed by other people's achievement and success but unwilling to take the path that led to their success. Many want the shortcuts to success. We see marriages that have lasted over five decades and we want that. But the journey is not going to be smooth all the way. There are times when the bed will be full of thorns rather than roses. It's all part of the process to get to success. It is essential that we lay the right foundation for our lives and marriage.

Some of us may need to start tearing some things apart and start rebuilding because we want a better house and may have been using inferior materials. Some of us may have realized we need a deeper foundation. For some of us, there are some things we cannot undo. Some mistakes are costly and irrevocable. For many, we cannot regain those times and opportunities we have lost, but thank God for second chances. I believe that as long as there's life, there's hope. So, we can all start from somewhere. Don't give up on yourself! The journey is not over!

Pillars are also very important parts of a building. Pillars are supporting structures. Every building must have pillars to be able to withstand any external forces. There are many pillars that hold up a marriage, but I'll only mention and analyze four, Respect, Understanding, Forgiveness and Sacrifice.

Respect

Also known as honor, reverence, appreciation. It is so crucial that both spouses respect each other. Respect is not a one-way stream. Some will say, respect is reciprocal. When you respect someone, you do not want to step on their toes or offend them. We want the person we respect to think highly of us, and so we do not misbehave around them. We don't act rudely, or untowardly or in an unbecoming manner towards a person we respect. Respecting someone means we place a certain level of value on that person, we do not look down on that person, we hold them in high esteem or regard. When couples respect each other, they do not do things that offends the other person, they do not act rudely towards each other, and they value each other's opinions and thoughts.

Respect is elicited by virtue of who the other person is to us and what they mean to us. If we place value on ourselves, we would respect our spouses, because they are an extension of who we are. If we treat our spouses worthlessly, we are indirectly inferring that we're worthless as well.

Respect is so crucial that lack of it leads to many problems in a marriage. Lack of reverence for their spouse is what causes some to cheat. Lack of honor for each other is what leads spouses to publicly embarrass or humiliate each other.

Traditionally, respect is very important to men. But I daresay it is just as important to women, although respect for women in heterosexual relationships has been **relegated** to a back seat for so long. Which is why many men do not consider respect as a virtue they should demonstrate to their wives. But I speak for myself and many women when I say respect is just as important to the wife as it is to the husband. Do not claim to love somebody when you do not respect them, that makes no sense. If we truly love our spouses, then we'll treat them deferentially.

People have different respect languages, just like there are different love languages. We have to learn the ways in which our spouses wish to be respected.

In my culture, respect for some means using honorifics when addressing them. For some, it means staying faithful to them and not flirting with others or sleeping around. For some, it means how you treat them, their family and friends. For some, it is a combination of all these elements and more. To me personally, respect means you care about how your actions affect me, so you don't do things that upset me. It means you value my thoughts and opinions and you don't disregard them.

Part of showing respect is showing appreciation to our spouse, not taking them for granted, and not trifling with them. I get so mad when I see couples take each other for granted. I looked up the meaning of the expression and it states, "fail to properly appreciate (someone or something), especially as a result of over-familiarity." Over-familiarity with our spouses sometimes makes us not value them as we ought to. We can become so familiar with them we don't appreciate or respect them as much as we used to.

During the dating phase of a relationship, before couples get married, they pull all the stops for their partner, guys especially. That woman becomes their bae (before all else) for real. Anything she wants, she gets; time, attention, money, you name it. Before she calls, they answer.

But often after marriage, because they figured they already "have her in the bag" and she isn't going nowhere, the intensity of the affection they used to show begins to dwindle. After marriage, some couples no longer pay attention to each other like they used to. Those sweet and affectionate words no longer come as freely and easily as they used to. Now the woman has to call several times before she's answered. That's when she has to beg to spend time with her. Where is the love? We are responsible for keeping the fire burning in our marriage!

Don't ever stop dating! Even after the nuptials, you have to keep dating your spouse!

Understanding

In many cases, communications is listed as one of the top reasons couples divorce. Communications skills are so vital to have when dealing with other people. You do not need to know how to communicate if you lived in a forest or an island all by yourself, but as long as you have contacts and interactions with other humans, it's a skill you cannot do without.

The verbals are just as important as the nonverbals; the body languages, the facial expressions, and the inflections. We need to know these things, especially when it comes to our spouses. A person can say, "you can go," when in fact what he or she is saying is "you better not take a step out of that door." We need to learn how our partner communicates. It is one thing to communicate; it is another thing to understand what is being communicated, from what perspective it is being communicated and with what intentions the message is being conveyed. We need to understand our spouses in order to grasp from what angle they are communicating at any given time.

If there is no understanding, there will be constant conflict. A simple and innocent statement can be misconstrued as having an ulterior motive. Sometimes, we see people flip out over little things, and we wonder, "I really didn't mean it like that, I didn't mean to offend her, she took it the wrong way." Of a truth, the intention may have been different, but the receiver took it the wrong way.

A husband can say to his wife, "Darling I think you are putting on a little bit of weight." It could be just an observation, nothing more, but she could misconstrue his intentions. Just picture this dialogue between a husband and wife:

Husband: Darling, I think you're putting on some weight, maybe we should cut back on the soda.

Wife: So, you're calling me fat now? Didn't you see me before you married me? What about you with your bald head and pot belly? So, you are saying you no longer find me attractive?

Husband: No, that's not what I'm saying. I still think you're very beautiful woman.

Wife: But obviously not beautiful enough for you. If you don't like me there are many men out there who appreciate me just the way I am; I don't need none of this.

And so, it goes on and on and on. This scenario may seem funny or disturbing, but it is very realistic. In many cases, simple things lead to misunderstanding in marriages.

But understanding our spouses is not limited to communications alone. We have to understand who they are, how they think, what makes them angry, their limitations, their strengths, their weakness, their preferences, their love language, what makes them happy, and what makes them tick. All these things and so on and so forth.

The opposite of understanding is misunderstanding also known as misinterpretation, misconception, misconstruction, misapprehension, disagreement, dispute, argument, and quarrel. Each of these words connote different meanings all of which can ensue between couples when there is no understanding.

Forgiveness

Not holding onto grudges and learning to let go of offenses is so important because your spouse will most definitely step on your toes. Offenses will come. For many diverse reasons, different kinds of offenses will arise. Remember you are two different people coming together to try to form a unit. You are trying to merge all these elements together: different gender, different background, different upbringing, and in some cases different culture and religion. Expect that there will be some clashes and difference of opinions. Even those we grow up with, like our family and friends often offend and hurt us. We cannot always expect our spouses to get it right. We must learn to forgive and keep no record of wrong.

Unforgiveness will only inhibit the relationship from progressing. Things will happen, things can happen, people make mistakes and we all have weaknesses. Part of loving somebody is deciding to overlook their shortcomings. Don't get stuck in past wrongs. Don't hold yourself a prisoner to unforgiveness and bitterness. Be free!

Sacrifice

Sacrifice is one of the lifelines of a good marriage! Marriage involves two persons so you're going to have to give up the I for us. We can no longer do things without taking the other person into consideration. We have to factor our spouses into our decision making. Being Miss and Mr. Independent before we get married is awesome! It's one of the best titles we could hold as singles. But once married, it simply cannot exist anymore. We are no longer independent of each other. Your actions affect mine and mine affects yours. Goals and visions becomes a shared goal and a shared vision. In marriage, you cannot be self-centered and be all about yourself, that's the sacrifice you are going to have to make for love.

In a marriage, you give up the me for the us. You do things that benefit not just only you but the other person as well. You do not do things that are convenient for you alone. If you want to live your life with only you at the center of your world, then please remain single. Marriage means putting someone else before you.

I encourage single folks to sow their wild oats. Do whatever it is you can do as a single person, explore and have fun. But keep in mind that our actions have consequences. I encourage this because when you get into marriage, it's time for you to be responsible for not just yourself but another person. You can still pursue your dreams after you get married, but not at the expense of the other person. A dream or goal that affects the other person's security and stability is best left alone. There has to be a mutual agreement in the pursuit of goals. This is why it's so very crucial that you're both going in the same direction, that your values and visions align. A house divided against itself cannot stand.

You don't want a situation whereby you're trying to get to the top (whatever that means to you), and the other person is pulling you down. You don't want a situation whereby you are both supposed to be chasing ten thousand together but instead you are individually chasing a thousand separately. Instead of the ten thousand God promised, you have two thousand because you are not working together! Sacrifice is very important, but it means accomplishing something together. I repeat, we have to give up the I for the us.

We have seen cases whereby mothers or fathers give up some opportunities, just so they can be there for their children, so their children can have the best. Parents work so very hard all for the future of their young ones.

My parents say this to my siblings and me all the time, the reason why we are in American hustling and all of that, is because of you guys. We could be back in Nigeria living our lives, we are landlords, we can have drivers and maids and be living that life, but we are sacrificing, so you guys can get good education and be better than us, because our joy and true fulfillment as parents is to see our children get to their destiny.

The joy and fulfillment of your spouse is to see you reach your destination in life, to be your cheerleader every step of the way, to believe in you and to see you get there. Because your success is your spouse's success, your accomplishment is their accomplishment; your accolades is their accolades, vice versa.

CHAPTER 11: A NOTE FROM ME TO YOU

I find that the more I write, the better I get at it. One thing I've learned about myself through writing is that I lack patience. Once I get an inspiration for a post, I want to quickly write and put it out there. I don't take enough time to edit and proofread. I catch my own errors days after I already published a post. I get mortified by the simple mistakes that I really shouldn't be making because I fail to properly proofread. But I have gotten better with time. I'm in no way close to being a perfect writer if there is such a thing. However, I do know I'm well on my way to mastering the art of writing because I have not stopped writing. Another realization I came to about myself is that I am a writer (writing this line made me laugh). *I am a writer.*

For a very long time, I refused to acknowledge that writing was one of my innate abilities. When people would refer to me as a writer, I would say, *no I'm not a writer, I'm just a person who writes.* I did not do this out of false modesty. On the contrary, I just did not see myself as a writer. I took English classes and writing intensive classes in college but never an actual writing class. I wish I had taken a class in creative writing. In fact, I wish I had majored in English, that would have made me a more proficient writer. I majored in Communications instead. But the more I write, the more I become more comfortable with the title.

When I go back to read my words, I almost can't believe I wrote them. Sometimes, I sit for hours feeling very impressed with myself because I just did not know I had it in me. We all have those kinds of moments in our lives when we get that satisfying feeling at having accomplished something great. Imagine how happy you'll feel if you succeed at making your marriage work? Especially when the odds are stacked against you. We all get frustrated and discouraged by our failures. We sometimes have the mindset of, "if they failed at it what chances do I have?" Well, you'll never know if you never try. But what if I fail? I read somewhere that FAIL means "First Attempt in Learning." Every failure is a learning curve. Try again and keep trying until you get it right. This is how many people became successful. You'll never succeed if you quit.

I learned that it takes ten years to master an act and realized that if I never start at all or if I don't keep at what I started, I'll never master it. Perhaps you are on the verge of giving up on your marriage, or you have already given up, why not start again and keep at it this time? Be intentional about making it work. You will get better at it the more you put in practices and habits that make a marriage work. You'll learn a lot about yourself along the line, the qualities/skills you already have in the bag, and ones you need to work on. But one thing is guaranteed, you'll not remain the same because you are taking steps towards a better you.

Why Do Marriages Fail

One of the most memorable blog posts I've written is the one I wrote on why marriages fail. The title to most of my write-ups on relationships is written in form of a question. The reason being that I write them to find answers to some of the questions that plague me.

Sometimes, I answer these questions myself and sometimes I pose the questions to readers instead. In this particular post, I asked, "why do marriages fail?" This must have truly resonated with quite a number of people because I received many feedbacks afterwards. They came mostly from married and divorced couples and a few single folks whose relationships have failed. A particular young man whose engagement was broken that same month I wrote the blog was very touched that he reached out to me to share his story.

I had written in the blog that marriages fail because couples choose to stop loving each other. A reader once told me that I was skillful at oversimplification when I write. A number of readers have told me it's not as simple as that. While writing a blog post does not allow for deep analysis (I just want to get a point across as succinctly as possible), on this particular issue of why marriages fail, I believe it is as simple as that.

I understand that multiplicity of factors can lead to the failure of a marriage, but I maintain that it can all be summarized into this one sentence, "Marriages fail because couples choose to stop loving each other." There's a keyword in this sentence to take note of and that is the word CHOOSE.

We sometimes underestimate the power of choices. But as humans, this is perhaps the most powerful apparatus we possess. Choice, the ability to choose. Everything we will ever amount to in life is based on the choices we make. Our final destiny is the sum total of our decisions. We can predict how a person's life will turn out years from now by the choices they make.

It's logical. Take for instance, a person refuses to quit smoking, after the doctors warned of the health risks; smoking is toxic to the body, it's damaging to internal organs. If this smoker does not stop, he or she may end up like one of those people on those horrible TV commercials on smoking. Those ads are so terrible I can't even watch them. But the reality is despite those ads, many people still smoke. That's the power of choice.

In the case of marriage, while divorce may not necessarily lead to a physical death, it signifies the death of so many things, the death of a union, a promise, a vow, and most of all the death of love. We have heard people make expressions like "we just grew apart," as if growing apart is something that happens by itself without a human agent fueling the process either by their actions or inactions.

People don't just grow apart. By not taking steps to grow closer, they have taken steps to become distant to each other. Either way, an action is being effectuated. Therefore, when a marriage fails, (grow apart, divorce, separation, infidelity), it did not just happen. In many cases, it takes a very long time for issues to completely get out of hands, but couples fail to manage the problem from the early stages before it escalates or plummets. They did not do something about it, which in and of itself is an action, *a choice.*

We take it for granted that our love will last forever, that things will just somehow work themselves out while we refuse to take necessary actions. It's like a student trying to pass an exam, without attending lectures or studying. How can such a student show up in the examination hall and expect to get an A? He may get lucky by some fluke of nature, but the odds are definitely stacked against him and I bet he won't keep getting lucky all the time. My point is, we have to put in the effort to make our marriage work and this goes back to all I've written so far.

Love will not last forever if we do not make deliberate decisions to make it last. If a husband keeps cheating on his wife hoping that her love for him will continue to save the marriage, while that may work for a while, after a period of time, that woman's love will die because he keeps choking it. Yes, love can die!

What keeps love alive is our actions. If we keep doing things to kill love, it will die. Love does not sustain itself. Love is a verb. A verb is an action word. An action requires that someone performs it. Marriages fail when partners refuse to perform their duties. It is not enough for one person to make all the right moves without the participation of the other person. The two partners involved have to work together. That's just how it is.

What actually inspired this blog post on why marriages fail was a conversation I had with a friend who had just gone through a divorce. The reason surprisingly was not infidelity, it wasn't money, it was boredom. It was my first-time hearing that a person divorced because she was bored.

At first it sounded ridiculous (it still does) but believe it or not it happened. A woman packed and left her husband and children because she was bored, and she figured she'd have more fun and excitement living as a single person than with her husband and kids. This happened after ten years of marriage. This was the story that inspired the blog post.

This couple for one reason or the other failed to keep their love alive. Now some may say, I will never divorce over such a trivial matter. But I present to you that there are many people who choose to remain in a marriage where they are miserable and unfulfilled. That is just as bad.

Using this couple as a case study, I began thinking of how similar couples out there could have kept the fire burning. I discovered that simple acts and deeds are what we take for granted the most. I began thinking of ways in which partners can please and keep each other happy, and I noticed that the little things count.

These minor things we underestimate in relationships; I refer to as adornments. Still using my analogy of a house, we can think of them as the painting of the house, they are the furniture, the decorations and the finishing touches.

These little things are so important! They make the house beautiful and give it a complete look/feel. Think about those house interiors we see in architectural magazines. We don't admire them for the bricks and blocks or the walls and polls. We don't care about none of that. What catches our attention is the design, the color, how everything is arranged and assembled, and how it all comes together to create a beautiful aesthetic.

When we picture our dream houses, they don't come up as empty spaces. Some of us are so imaginative that we specify such things as the color of the rugs and doormats. These things may be considered minor, but a wrong color combination can turn a fine house into an ugly one, a hideous cotton can totally alter the appearance of a room.

In a marriage, adornments are those little things couples do to stay romantic. It is the idea of dating after marriage which I mentioned briefly earlier. As time goes on, it's possible for a marriage to become a routine, familiar and boring. How do we spice things up? How do we switch things around without going overboard? You do not need a ridiculously expensive vacation to keep a marriage exciting! By all means, please take a vacation once in a while when you can afford it. Go ahead and spoil yourself, go on several honeymoons.

I am a sucker for romantic movies and great movie lines. If one stands out to me, I don't ever forget it. This line, "Just because it's Wednesday," from the movie *Juwanna Mann* is one of my favorites. Vivica Fox's character in the movie talked about how she wishes a man will just buy roses for a woman not just on valentine's day or a holiday or birthday as they typically do, but just because it's Wednesday. It's the idea of not sticking to convention but being spontaneous. I find this deeply romantic because it's unexpected. The element of surprise makes it so sweet. Who says you only have to buy flowers for her on holidays? Who says you always have to do things the way you've always done them?

Lovebirds, when was the last time you took each other on a date? Like one of those ones you used to have before you got married? I know there are responsibilities, kids and all of that, but you have to create time for your partner!

Find little ways to do little things that would put a smile on the other person's face and touch their heart so very deeply. Find simple ways to show them you still care, you're thinking about them, you love them, and you appreciate them. Be inventive and creative. There are tons of information out there on how to spice up your sex life and your marriage. These little things can go a long way in saving your marriage.

CHAPTER 12: SOME FAVORITES POSTS FROM MY BLOG

I am always encouraged when strangers approach me to tell me about how my writing has helped them in one way or the other or simply that they loved my writing style or unique perspective. It gives a deep sense of satisfaction to know that in my own little way, I am making a difference. As I bring an end to this book, I'd like to include some of the posts that has gained the most traction on my blog. Enjoy!

All You Need is Love and Then Some

It takes more than love to make a relationship work. The older I grow, the more I realize I have been lied to. All those Mills &

Boon romantic novels I read as a teenager could not have in any way prepared me for real life experiences of relationships. It dawned on me that I was deceived by Hollywood as well, happily ever after is not always so happy after couples walk off the isle. Oh, don't get me started on all those love songs, I'm so sick of them. They in no way encompass the ups and downs and intricacies of relationships. In short, all they describe as love does not make a relationship work! Love and romance work well in the imaginary space created by writers and producers, but the real world is nothing like we read in novels.

In the real world, you need more than love to make a relationship successful. This is what romance novels and movies do not tell us. It takes more than falling in love to sustain a marriage. Love, the kind of love described in books and movies is not enough to make a relationship flourish. If all we truly need is love, then 50% of marriages will not end in divorce. Love could not be the only recipe for the other 50% that seem to be doing fine. Yes, love is important, but it takes more than love or rather it takes more than the emotion of love to make a marriage work.

A successful marriage requires knowledge, knowing how to live with people, knowing the differences between a man and a woman, knowing how to deal with finances, knowing how to communicate, knowing when to shut up and knowing when to speak, knowing how to be self-controlled, knowing how to express yourself, knowing how to read people, etc. These seemingly little things break marriages, not lack of love. An abusive man may still claim to love his wife. It could be very well true that he feels those emotions for her. He could still "love" her but lack the ability to control his anger. A person who cheats on his spouse could very much still "love" the spouse but lack the ability to control his sexual appetites. Infidelity, abuse, and lack of financial management have broken homes; this is not because the couples do not love each other, but because they lack the proper knowledge of what makes a marriage work.

People need to stop going into marriage because they fell in love. Situations will arise that are stronger than that feeling, then what happens? You could give yourself a fighting chance by acquiring knowledge. I wish there was a school for love and marriage because every single person needs to enroll and learn.

I mentioned in an earlier post that "irreconcilable differences" has become such a cliché for couples getting a divorce these days. Well if only they knew that in addition to falling in love, they also need to connect emotionally, maybe they wouldn't have gone into the marriage in the first place. In addition to falling in love, you need deep emotional connection; this entails that you connect romantically, intellectually, socially, behaviorally, financially, and economically.

There is what is called emotional intelligence (EI). This is the backbone of all you will ever achieve as a person. If there is low EI then there is no capacity and therefore nothing to fill, which results in suboptimal output. "Suboptimal" refers to something less than the highest standard. Your marriage will be less than the highest standard if you lack emotional intelligence. While some are born with enviable EI, most is learned (acquired). So, connecting in all the above-mentioned ways requires intelligence. Or put differently, knowledge! We need to acquire the knowledge of what marriage entails and how to make it succeed.

It is not wise to want to cook a meal without first counting the cost and making sure you have the right ingredients, enough ingredients or enough money to buy the ingredients required. If you go ahead and prepare it, the dish will end up coming out as something entirely different from the idea you had in mind and once it's done, there may be nothing you can do to reverse it. You may choose to throw it away and start all over again, or you may choose to eat it like that, or you may choose to add some other ingredients to make it better. This is what a marriage is like; it's like a dish. It's never going to come out perfectly until you have the right ingredients and until you know how to apply the right ingredients to make it superb. There are no perfect marriages because there are no perfect people. However, there are great and successful marriages, and the key ingredient is knowledge.

Why Am I Still Single?

Is a question many of us single ladies are asking ourselves. Some women have already resigned themselves to the fate of solitariness. They have settled for endless dating that never yields permanency, sex with strangers now and then, an empty crib with nothing but cats to snuggle up with, and marriage to a career that will never bring full fulfillment. But some of us want more! We want biceps and triceps to cuddle up with in bed every night (not cats!). We want commitment; we want love, we want relationship, we want to share not just our bodies but our minds and deepest thoughts with another person, and we want a partner for life. If you've ever seen any woman or girlfriend get married to a "perfect" guy and you wonder what in the world is going on? I know I'm better than her (it's not being boastful, it's just a fact). If you're that person, then this blog is for you. Every year, we see friends and acquaintances get married before our eyes, and sometimes, we are bridesmaids. And we wonder when is it ever going to be my turn? When is that perfect gentleman going to waltz in? Why am I still single?! I'm beautiful; I have an education, I have a car, I have a career, I have my money, but, where is he?

Well, the answers to those questions can be endless, so I'll only address a critical area that we may overlook. I'll ask a question of my own, do you have a list? If the answer is yes, then keep reading. If the answer is no (which is highly unlikely), then feel free to stop reading at this point. Now to my beautiful dames with the list of what the perfect man should be, I have only a few words for you —**trash that list**. Yes, throw it in the garbage. Be it a physical or mental catalog of what you want in a man; it is one of the reasons why you're still single. I'm not asking you to decimate your standards; I'm only saying to reassess them.

If physique is still a criterion for pass or fail anywhere in your prospectus, then scrap it. There are many great men out there who are as short as Kevin Hart. I understand that we are attracted to certain kinds of physical traits, but let's face it, the right person for us may not have six packs. Furthermore, you may be too high-maintenance. You may need to lower some of your expectations, particularly those that are materially inclined. Now my advice may be sounding subdued, since we live in a generation that is all about being true to who you are. Some may say, that is just how I roll. On one hand this is great, but perhaps this is why we have so many quandaries in this generation. As we are asking people to be true to who they are when who they are is messed up! Many people do not have character. Some folks are so materialistic and vain. Rather than teach them how to be decent human beings, we encourage all sort of unsavory conducts all in the name of freedom. I find that liberty has become licentiousness in this age.

There is now a blurred line between what's right and proper and what's downright ignoble. Therefore, each and every one of us will have to make a choice.

Do you want marriage? Do you want commitment and long-lasting love? Then you're going to have to choose it. Alas, gone are the days when these things come easily. Today, the world provides us with many illusorily enticing alternatives. We'll have to cast the ballot for what is not only right but good. Marriage is good! I am not saying this to vilify singleness, but don't get it twisted; marriage is one of the greatest fulfillment we humans can have. You're probably reading this post because you're tired of being single, so we may as well be honest with ourselves. Having a spouse who is forever in your corner tops sex on a regular with someone who will never commit to you. The right person for you may not appear anywhere on that treasured checklist and that's possibly why you're still single. So, obliterate that superficial list and be open, (but not too open), and you may just see him walk right through the door.

Ìwà lẹwà (Character is Beauty)

Ìwà lẹwà is a saying in the Yoruba language that I did not quite understand until recently. There are many such similar proverbs. The Yoruba people pride themselves on being well cultured, and full of deep ancestral wisdom. There is always an idiom, proverb or folklore readily available to be applied to any circumstance. There are proverbs for wayward children and also for dutiful ones. There are several proverbs for a good person and similarly for an evil person. For every human experience, behavior or circumstance, there is a proverb in Yoruba that can be applied. Hardly will the elders make a statement without it being inclusive of some adage or words of wisdom. It's a privilege to be a part of such rich ancestral and cultural heritage.

Ìwà lẹwà, is a very common saying among Yorubas. It literally means character is beauty and is used to speak well of women who are not facially attractive but have a good character or to speak ill of women who are beautiful but have an evil character. Being a woman born and raised in Yoruba land, I understood the literal meaning of the words, but the wisdom of it eluded me until recently.

I was having a very candid exchange with a Nigerian male friend. He's the kind I would refer to as matured, exposed and full of wisdom based on experience, and several years of learning. I have known him for quite a while and have engaged in many intellectual dialogue with him, so I trusted his wisdom and judgment. I don't recall exactly how we came around to discussing the topic of women and beauty, but I remember telling him how I thought it was not fair that it is still socially unacceptable for women to propose. Being the feminist that I am, I can hardly converse with the opposite sex without introducing the subject of gender roles. But he disagreed with me and in fact made a statement that I thought radical. He said, not only can and do women propose, it has always been a woman's call.

And so, on a cold winter night, sitting on our respective couches enjoying a late-night banter as we wait for sleep to envelope us, we began our didactic explication of the intricate relationship between a man and a woman. Like a leaved tree, the conversation branched off into different directions one of which is the concept of women, character and beauty.

I remember my friend saying something to the effect of, "I'm going to be very raw with you right now." Having spent so much time in engaging with men, I understood this was a code for giving away some male secrets that women aren't often aware of. Therefore, I knew to sit up and pay close attention. I'm a bit of an enthusiast when it comes to learning, particularly when the subject involves the opposite sex, their peculiar ways and how they think in relations to women. While, I do not entirely endorse the idea of thinking like a man, I do believe it is critical to understand how men think. So, with my ears perked up like an eager pupil ready to learn, my dear friend began his insightful lecture.

Women are responsible for initiating the proposal process. While they may not overtly go on one knee to pop the question as men do, a woman proposes to the man that she wants to marry him by investing her character into the union. A woman who has no interest in settling down with a man will not invest her moral qualities into the relationship. Let's take for instance, a side chick. She is in the affair for the money and the pleasure. She has no reason to behave in a wifely manner. A side chick who begins to act like a wife is getting ready to take over.

When a woman demonstrates through her disposition that she is interested in building a home with a man, then he goes down on one knee and proposes. But a woman in which he does not perceive a good character (or as some will say, a wife material), he may play around with, but will never commit to. Because once a man gets past the sex phase of the relationship, whether or not he sleeps with the woman, the only thing keeping him is her character.

The first thing that attracts a man is a woman's physical appeal. Don't be deceived, no matter how "holy" he claims to be, all men are drawn to the same thing, the looks, the butt, and the boobs. When a man sees a woman he fancies, the first thing that comes to mind is sex. Not her intellect, success, moral standard or personality. If he succeeds in getting her to bed before any real attachment is formed, he's bound to lose interest. If we cover up the faces of all women and expose their nakedness, underneath the clothing, vaginas are all the same. So, what keeps a man is not a woman's sexual allure, there's always a woman more beautiful than the current one. Men who do not act on their natural impulse mostly hold back for four reasons; self-control, respect for their spouses, love for their children and their personal convictions. Take those four away and all men will cheat. Don't you ever think you can keep a man with your physical beauty? The true charm lies in your character.

Some women at the beginning of the romance pulls the man in with a good character, and then later flips on him by displaying a bad one. This often results in the man cheating or the relationship falling apart. A woman who cannot hold her man with her good conduct, is no different from every other woman out there batting their false lashes at him. This is the true meaning of Ìwà lẹwà.

However, some men will still cheat regardless of how good the woman is. This is because it's a natural impulse and he has not learned to have self-control. Or simply because he is a jerk. But the point is a woman's character is more attractive than her physical beauty.

I was pleased with this response. I like the idea of subtly proposing to a man. Many of us have too much female pride to begin with. We do not really want to go down on one knee and ask a man to marry us, no matter how crazy we are about him.

If we pride ourselves on our outer beauty, there's always a woman more seductive around the corner and there's no guarantee that if you got him by your beauty, another woman cannot take him away by hers. A real man sees past the outer covering, the make-up and the false lashes to the soul within which is revealed by our character either good or bad. While, it is essential to beautify the outside, we must not fail to build our character as well. This is our true beauty as women.

When the Thrill is Gone

"What about mad love and undying passion?" "Affection and comfortable lust are better." Vanessa Grant, *If You Loved me*.

I was reading a romance novel when I came across these lines. I haven't picked up a romantic book in a while, but they are my go to when I need the assurance that true love does exist. Whether in fiction or real life, it matters not. What is central is that if the human mind can conjure up such passion as we encounter on the pages of a good book, then surely it must be within our means to attain it. This conclusion is all the comfort I needed as I face my own reality as a single woman living in the real world.

Mad love and undying passion versus affection and comfortable lust, which one is better? This question I grappled with after I read those lines from a dialogue between a man and a woman he is romantically involved with. The woman in question is our romance heroine, while her partner is the man she has been passively dating for a couple of months. It's no surprise that women are the more sentimental ones. We all want the crazy love and the fiery passion, that is just how we are designed. Women are emotional feelers, while men are logical thinkers. That is not to say women cannot be rational and men emotional, but some traits are more dominant in one sex than the other.

As I contemplated these extremes, mad love versus affection, undying passion versus comfortable lust, emotions versus rationality, women versus men, I surmised that one is not necessarily superior to the other. Of course, our natural inclination is to place mad love above affection, and undying passion above comfortable lust since one appears to be more intense than the other. But I propose that they are not necessarily antipodes, but rather an extension of the other. Paradoxically, I would argue that relationships built on the idea of affection and comfortable lust, last longer than those built on the idea of mad love and undying passion. If research is true, then couples we are looking to have a long-lasting relationship ought to discard the notion of mad love and undying passion altogether.

But we often do not think about the length as much as we think about the depth when it comes to love and relationships. A lot of emphasis is placed on feelings rather than longevity. We are obsessed with how the other person makes us feel, the tingling sensation in our chest, the butterflies in our stomach, the goosebumps on our arms, and all those other delicious things they do to us. These are all wonderful and great; we should feel this way, we deserve to feel this way, every single human being in a romantic relationship ought to experience these pleasurable sensations! But after these feelings, then what?

The romance novels fail to tell us that this delightful tenderness will not last forever. While they assure us that crazy love, fervent ardor, and strong desire do exist, they never tell us what happens to our heroes and heroines after they dash off into the sunset on their white horses. We are left believing it is truly all happily ever after when we close the last page on the final chapter. The writers are so good; they leave us desiring the kind of love we witnessed on those cream-colored pages. Our reality seems pale in comparison. If you've ever read a good romance novel, then you know exactly what I'm talking about. But I've become skilled at piecing apart fiction from reality. Attribute this to years of living in the real world. Soon enough, some of us wake up from fairytale land or are hijacked from it when reality sets in. Nothing wakes us up faster than a broken heart, and most of us have experienced that. If you haven't experienced a broken heart, you have not yet lived.

Back to my question, what happens after the feelings are gone? Oh yes, they'll vanish sooner or later. Research reveals that in the early stages of a romantic relationship the critical part of our brains takes a vacation, while all these sex and bonding hormones go to work (testosterone, dopamine, and oxytocin). But soon enough, the critical part of our brains returns, and the chemicals are put to rest. Clinical Psychologist, Mona Fishbane, explains it best in an online post, she writes, "At some point the critical part of the brain come back online, and we see our partners, warts and all. The jazzed-up chemicals settle down, and our drug high gives way to a calmer brain state." At this point, couples can either decide to have an affair, divorce and remarry or settle into a life of affection and comfortable lust. The stage of mad love and undying passion last between a year and three years. Those who stay together are those who have factored this fact into the relationship from the onset. The idea of mad love and undying passion conveyed to us by romance novels is quaint and charming, but it does not last forever. Let's be realistic; there is no such thing as undying passion. Biology will eventually take its course; our brains cannot keep up with all those euphoric chemicals forever.

So, I decided that I wanted both mad love and "undying" passion and when that is gone, affection and comfortable lust with my partner. Now this idea may not sound too romantic, but I believe that there is beauty in longevity. Whether a marriage is sustained by mad love and later affection or solely by affection throughout the lifespan of the couple, the crucial factor is that it is sustained. I would choose an affectionate marriage with a satisfactory level of lust over a broken one on any day.

I have seen couples who keep reinventing ways to recreate the chemicals and keep the romance sizzling after many years of marriage, and couples we are perfectly contented with their easy affection towards each other. It is entirely up to us to make our marriage what we desire for it to be, or to cast it away when the thrill is gone.

When the Going Gets Tough

Lately, I have met a lot of happy and interesting people. These are people who in spite of their sad situations have chosen to be happy. I've laid emphasis on the word "chosen," for happiness is a choice. I consider myself privileged to have people (virtually strangers) confide in me about some of their most painful circumstances, particularly the failure of a relationship. Each and every one of us, even the most conservative of us have experienced this at one time or another (except for those lucky few), and there are varying degrees of distraughting emotions that take place depending on the level of attachment. For instance, a divorce may be more traumatic than a broken engagement. We all enter into a relationship with the expectation that it would work out. No one hopes or wishes for it to end. Even about to-be-wedded couples muttering the words "for better, for worst" with all the emotions and feelings they could muster, do not really expect that things would turn out for the worst. But they sometimes do. We only need to look around us to see that. You and I know at least one or two divorced couples, or a couple who is about to take the plunge.

What happened? This is the first question I often ask. Some of these folks are ready to divulge even before I ask. I guess there's a certain ease when it comes to opening up to complete strangers that stems from the notion that they don't know us, and our parts may never cross with theirs again, so we are reassured that our secrets are safe with them. What happened? The answers vary from one gender to another, one situation to the next, and one status to another (married, engaged or dating), depending on the level of commitment, how long the relationship lasted, how long ago it ended, how it ended, and who called it off. I analyze each of these cases and try to determine if some the couples could have somehow worked it out. The plain and sad truth after my careful analysis is that they possibly couldn't have. I observed that no one truly desires for his or her romantic relationship to end.

Now I know we often think divorced couples could have stayed married. We believe there is got to be a way to make it work or they gave up too easily. Unfortunately, this is not often the case. Most people see marriage as that bridge of no return, once couples have crossed it, they are expected to remain in it for the rest of their lives. That's a great outlook to have on marriage. Otherwise, what really sets it apart from other romantic relationships that are more or less treated as a drive-through? We should have that expectation of "together ever after" in a marital union, and happily too. But sadly, it is not always so clear-cut.

Now I am not advocating for divorce. It is not the ideal situation for anyone, but it ends up happening anyways, due to a number of different reasons. But it does not have to. In all of the cases I've been privy to, be it a broken engagement, a divorce, or a dissolvement of a long relationship, what I have come to learn is that no matter the circumstances of the dissolution or the reason each person is giving as to why the union ended, it mostly boils down to this one factor, change. Ever heard of the phrase "this is not the person I married?" What is simply being said is that the person changed and seemed almost like a different person. After a relationship crashes or is about to, we would often hear things like "When I first met him, he was this or that, but then he began to change," Or "I don't know who she is anymore." People change, and circumstances change and sometimes we do not know how to deal with them.

Many people entering into a lifetime commitment fail to grasp the implication of what it is to be with a human being— a living, breathing, autonomous agent with a mind, body and soul. I think we too often underestimate human beings, and what ends up happening is that they do some things that catches us unaware or shocks us. But it would not if only we had been more intentional in our approach to the relationship. Sadly, people only tend to focus on the outer shell (body) that makes up a person; we make no inquiry into their interior, their minds and how they think.

People fall in love like leaves fall from trees and are swept off their feet just as the wind sweeps off those same leaves and the love crumbles and die just as the leaves do. We need to be more intentional with our relationship! Treat it like it is the most important mission you will ever embark on. Think of yourself as a soldier about to go to war, prepare for the unforeseen circumstances that may emerge. Expect people to change, anticipate issues that you do not even wish to deal with, (unfaithfulness, childlessness, lack of finances, illness, etc.) and be mentally and emotionally ready to deal with them. This is how a marriage lasts! I cannot overemphasize this; a relationship is as good as the two individuals involved. The sad reality is that often, two weak (lacking maturity or emotional intelligence, etc.) individuals come together in holy matrimony but ends up eating each other up like parasites, or a strong individual comes together with a weak one and that person ends up making his or her partner's live a series of unpleasant roller coaster rides. The perfect recipe for a solid and lasting relationship is for two whole individuals (mentally, emotionally, spiritually, etc.) to come together. Iron sharpens iron.

Back to my "she changed" or "he changed" people, more often than not, these people have been who they were from the beginning and have just evolved into a fuller version of themselves. We just did not see it because we were either blinded by love or because they pretended, and we did not have the discernment to see through the veil to who they truly are. But in some rare cases, a person can genuinely change, they could go from being good to being "bad". In situations like these, the two partners involved have to make the call on whether to keep the relationship going or to call it quit. It's a tough decision. Sometimes, one person wants to keep going and the other is at the end of his or her ropes. Besides, everyone has a mind of their own. No one can change anyone's mind unless the person is willing for his or her mind to be changed. A human's mind is the most difficult thing on earth to transform. This is what I mean by grasping the implication of what it is to be in a relationship with a human being. Your partner is a free-thinking agent. Who he or she really is, is what's covered up by the body. Stop getting carried away with the outer layer.

The questions we should ask ourselves then are, will I still love after this person does something hurtful I don't expect them to do? Will I love all the versions of this person to come? Will I love no matter what life throws at us? Will I stay for worst? This is where the choice comes in again. Love is a choice, but not one that can be made by just anyone. We do not need to be in a relationship to be happy or to live a fulfilling life. Marriage is a choice some people make. It takes the emotionally, spiritually, and mentally mature ones amongst us to stick to that choice through thick and thin, and good and worst. Unfortunately, a lot of people jump into relationships lacking these things and then bail out when the going gets tough.

The Best Quote I've Ever Heard About Love

Love isn't sacrificing something for the other person; it's accomplishing something _ (*It's Okay That's Love,* Jo In Sung.)

As a young woman in this contemporary society, there's a conscious side of me always pondering the question of what I would have to give up in order to live the kind of life my culture and society expects of me?

The other day a woman asked me what I was studying in college and what I intend to do with it. I don't get too thrilled when certain people ask me these questions, but I always try to give an honest answer. The woman listened on and appeared interested in my answer. I mentioned something about doing a lot of traveling and as I expected, I was immediately reminded that I am a woman and my biological clock was ticking or my night was getting darker (which was the phrase the woman used). I understood what she was saying; she meant I should drop my fancy notions and start thinking about marriage. In her opinion, it was going to be impossible for me to have the future I'm carving out for myself and have a successful family at the same time. And naturally family must come first because as women, we were raised from childhood with the mindset of having a family when we grow up.

While there's nothing wrong with aspiring towards marriage, it does reduces or even eliminates so many other possibilities of what a woman could do with her life. Often, women have had to give up their dreams and ambitions, so they could fit the mold society has dictated to them. I have thought it noble and very romantic in the past when I see women who were aspiring towards a big dream, suddenly give up that dream because they wanted to get married. I never questioned it because my culture elevates a woman sacrificing her ambitions for the sake of a man or her children.

But this quote made me think about it differently. Who says women can't have it all? All our dreams, ambitions, aspirations and a successful marriage. Why does a woman have to give up one for the other? Wouldn't men love it if their wives were overachievers in their chosen fields? Isn't that something to be proud of? Why does a woman's love have to mean giving up something? How about a love that accomplishes something?

I would love to see that kind of love. A love that dreams big and achieves big, a love that's not restricted by cultural expectations. But maybe it doesn't exist. I've seen it in Hollywood, but Hollywood is not the real world. My favorite quote about love is from a fictional character in a Korean drama I watched. That doesn't give me much hope, but one can certainly dream.

A Letter to Her Lover: Love is Not Enough

Dear Love,

If only love was all it took to make it work, then we wouldn't need patience, kindness, faith, endurance and perseverance. There will be no assumptions that I will meet your needs and you'll meet mine. We'll just come together to stay together with motives devoid of ego. Not needing assurance, a sense of security and comfort because all we need is love. We'd expect nothing in return for all we give because love has no expectations.

I would not expect you to call me back because I called you. I would not expect you to support me because I support you. I would not expect you to trust me because I trust you. I would not expect you to love me back because I love you. I would not expect you to be there, always and forever.

But we've both come to the realization that it takes more than love to make this thing called marriage work. It dawned on us that saying those four-letter words, three words sentence, eight-character alphabets does not guarantee trust, hope and forever. If anything, it means nothing. "I love you" does not mean, I will not break your heart, I will not cheat on you, I will not leave you. But still we toss it around, at times with feelings, but usually so casually. In the similar fashion we say, "I love chocolate" or "I love cars," we allege our love to each other, often without the awareness that those words invoke expectations. They conjure images of happiness, gold jewelries, champagne, roses, laughter, moonlight kisses, and forever.

We profess love perhaps in hope that it means we care so deeply for each other, so much so that there's no room for an interloper. Just I and you with nothing in between but love. Not I money and you, not I friends and you, not I family and you, not I ego and you, not I things and you, not I ambitions and you, but I love and you. I love you.

In naivety, we boldly declare it believing that is all it takes. We delude ourselves into thinking the Beatles were right when they sang *Love Is All You Need*, until we got married and we realized love is not enough, because if love was enough, it would keep us together. We found ourselves sinking, desperately trying to hold onto love thinking it is the anchor that will bring us ashore, but we found it not sufficient. Then we began to search for those other elements we needed to keep this ship afloat.

We searched for trust, but we couldn't find it. We searched for hope and it was missing. Faith eluded us. Sacrifice was nowhere to be. What about mutual respect, kindness, patience, acceptance, empathy, and courtesy? They were gone, if ever we had them. Then we thought to ourselves, what exactly is the use of love? And why do people place so much emphasis on it if it cannot even make this union last?

Then we concluded that love is useless. But that did not sound right, so we delved deeper and the deeper we burrowed we realized we knew nothing about love. How arrogant we were to think love is an intense feeling or a deep romantic and sexual attraction, so as long as we felt that tug of the heart, that tingling sensation on our skin, and that butterflies in our stomach, we thought we loved each other. But that is not love. What then is love? We asked. We looked to writers, poets, philosophers and composers for answers. But they all failed us. Then we realized love is not a thing that can be stumbled upon, or fallen into, "I fell in love" is one of the biggest flim-flams we ever invented. We don't fall into love like we fall into a pool, if anything, love is like little drops of water that takes years to turn into an ocean.

Love is a tree that grows and if only we have the patience to nurture it, we would see its fruits in due seasons. Love is not enough because it was still a seed when we started dating. We planted it when we got married, but that is only the beginning of a lifetime of sacrifice, endurance and perseverance.

But we give up too soon because love was not convenient. Yes, we got love, but what is love if it cannot keep us together forever? Love is nothing but an abstract.

I'm Choosing Love, Warmth in the Arms of My Lover and Matrimonial Bliss

It's already September! Before long, we'll be back to donning minks and gloves for winter. Isn't it amazing how time flies? Like a winged bird one moment it's there and the next it's gone.

I woke up one morning and it suddenly dawned on me that I am in a peculiar season in my life. Perhaps more interesting than any other seasons past. It's left to be seen what the years ahead have in store for me, but every season has its own unique peculiarities that makes it memorable. My entire childhood was spent in Nigeria and was filled with fun, cheerfulness and holy fervor. I was everyone's little princess, the smart, well spoken, out spoken and well-behaved one. Many of my activities involved church, I was in the adult choir and drama ministry, the only child who always attended Sunday school and never slept at vigils. Really a typical childhood for someone born into a conservative African Christian community. Part of my teenage years were spent in Nigeria, then I moved to the United States at sixteen. Teenagehood is not my favorite. I was plagued with all the insecurities, uncertainties and awkwardness of being a teenager combed with trying to figure out where I fit in in this strange and unfamiliar environment called America. But growing into a young adult and early twenties have been quite interesting so far for me. It's been a season of discoveries and accomplishments, and I'm beginning to get the hang of this thing called adulthood.

    I am quite pleased with what I've been able to complete so far. I may even receive a pat on the back for some of the accomplishments I already have in the bag (bachelor's degree, master's degree, career, extracurricular). Not bad for a young black girl some might say. But I often get restless and wonder if there's more to life than the obvious pattern I see my life falling into. As a matter of fact, life for most of us seem centered on these three coups, get an education, get a job, and get a husband or wife. That last part, I haven't quite gotten to yet, which makes this a very interesting season in my life, because at some point during this season, I am expected to accomplish that feat. Or so I've been convinced. Friends and family keep posing this question to me, what's left?

    What is left indeed? I have an education, I have a source of income, I now possess the qualities that qualify me for a husband, or do I? It sure sounds like it from the inordinate amount of pressure I get from society to get married. Whatever happened to exploring the world, building a dream and discovering yourself?

Those can all be done within the perimeters of your husband's house I'm told. And I'm often reminded of that notorious biological clock that keeps ticking.

When I was younger I used to have all these ideas about being a non-conformist, some kind of social rebel. Who says I have to get married and be tied to taking care of a man and some children for the rest of my life? How about dedicating my life to some charity or missionary cause somewhere in the world or a career or something, anything other than fulfilling that societal expectation of marriage? Now that I'm older, being a rebel just doesn't seem as appealing as it used to be. When I look around, I observe that all my friends are getting married, and the question remains what's left? Then it dawned on me that whether or not I get married, the question will remain.

There will always be more to life, more to explore, more to discover, more to experience and more to accomplish. Milestone after milestone, season after season there will be more to do with our lives than we already have, because time never stops and as long as we have the breadth of life, there will always be new heights to attain. Then I asked myself, isn't it better to go through life with a handsome someone as we both seek answer to that question, than to be a lonesome sojourner? And the answer was a soft and simple yes.

So, for this season, I'm choosing love, warmth in the arms of my lover and matrimonial bliss. May not sound as exciting as exploring the world, on the contrary it appears quite normative. But what I have discovered is that marriage is a deeply exhilarating adventurous journey in and of itself, if taken with the right partner. Someone who like yourself is ever restless, always eager to discover what's left. Who knows what cave of enchantments or treasures you may come upon as you both explore life together?

While seemingly normative, marriage is by no means ordinary or boring. It is more electrifying and stirring than any adventure we may seek in the alluring depths of the Grand Canyon or the highest peak of Mount Everest. What makes marriage seem unappealing to many in my generation is the complacency that steals over us, killing our quest for more. Marriage becomes bland and uninspiring when both individuals fail to keep up the hunt for life. Why should marriage be perceived as the end of fun and everything young folks look forward to? Why can't we have fun together with our spouses? I understand there are responsibilities (children, bills, etc.), but these should never stop us from enjoying life to the fullest. Marriage should be a thrilling journey of discoveries with our spouses. Sometimes, one spouse plays tour guide and at other times, the other takes over. But we should never stop exploring, never stop asking what's left and never stop seeking to discover it together.

What Makes Marriage Worth It?

May is such a special month for me. It's the month in which I am reminded of just how fast time is moving as I draw closer to old age. Time takes on a new significance for me, as I am reminded of how little of it I have to accomplish some of the feats that are expected of me before it's too late. I'm sure we all have ventures that we want to undertake before we reach a certain age or before we die. Be it ventures that we ourselves choose or ones that are chosen for us.

For most of us single women and men, marriage is the number one enterprise that has been chosen for us. We are expected to undertake this project at some point soon.

I was having a late-night conversation with a friend recently. It was of the reflective nature. My friend and I were just kicking it back on a warm spring night and we got talking about life and basically what's next? I just turned a new age; I am grateful to God for all I've been able to get done with my life so far. I don't take the privileges for granted. Marriage is unsurprisingly a common theme in many of my conversations with folks. I have been officially writing and talking about marriage for **over** two years now. But that aside, I am a young single individual, so it's not uncommon for marriage to come up a lot in my discussions with people.

As we were talking, my friend who was an equally single person said, "if I have a choice, I would not get married." And I responded that it was entirely up to him. It was his decision to make. At the end of the day, no one will actually drag him in black tuxedo to a court or a church, and no one will handcuff him to a woman. This was my response but if I was being honest, it's not quite as simple as that. While of a truth, singles are not being physically forced into marriage. The societal pressure is very real. It's just as dictatorial or forceful as being physically dragged to get married.

This theme of societal pressure is one that has gained a lot of traction of recent, especially among single women who are moving toward 30 or have passed it. 30 is referred to as the expiration date of a woman and I discovered that this cut across all cultures. All women have this in common, regardless of their race, or socioeconomics (income, education, occupation).

However, it seems as though men feel the pressure to get married as well. But more attention is focused on women's experiences. Perhaps thanks to the infamous biological clock. Biology teaches us that female fertility is affected by age. It's nature; we can't fight it. So, we must accept fate and endeavor to make hay while the sun shines. Unfortunately for many of us, it's not quite as simple as that. Many unforeseen circumstances can lead to delay in giving birth. One of which is getting married later, which itself can be caused by many other unforeseen circumstances.

However, people don't care to know our individual journeys or stories; they only want to see success, which often in their conclusion is marriage. I have said this several times before and I do believe it, more people will stay single if not for societal pressure to get married. I have entertained the thought of remaining single myself, but I'm not fit to be a rebel. I'm too much of a romantic.

With this strong conviction that many people will stay single if they have a choice, I began wondering what then makes marriage special and if it is indeed special, why would people opt out if they had a choice?

The answer was quite simple it's almost astounding in its simplicity. Love. Yes, love, that four-letter words is the answer. Love is what makes marriage special. Without love marriage is not worth it. If we trade love for other material things, then marriage really ain't worth nothing. Love should be the only motivation that will drive a single individual to give up his or her autonomy and freedom to be "shackled" down with another person. We must be crazy if we do it for any other reason than love! Because marriage is in a sense a prison. I don't mean to sound like a pessimist. Marriage could be a sweet prison, but not without love. So, love, that familiar cliché is what makes marriage special.

It's in marriage that people learn what love is, through caring for the other person and putting their needs first. It's really one of the greatest human accomplishments, the ability to love another human that is not your own flesh and blood. This is why marriage is worth it. And it's wrong to enter into the union with the mindset of what does the other person have to offer me? It should rather be, what do I have to offer the other person? It makes for the best of relationships when each individual come together with this mindset.

If we never become known as some of the famous people in the world, if we never invent something that puts our name on the map or accomplish a great feat, but have only learned to love and be loved, then we have fulfilled a great purpose on earth. If all we ever do is love someone, we can be wholeheartedly proud of ourselves.

Love stands in the same categories of other human successes. In fact, I believe it tops them all. It is most noble and not as publicized, but loving another human is one of the greatest feats we'll ever accomplish, for those who have been privileged with that opportunity.

Love is the most powerful force in the universe! We should all welcome the chance to be able to channel this force. It's a great honor indeed.

The Helpmate: For Singles and Married

I have been so focused on vlogging this month, I almost forgot to write. But writing remains my foremost passion and I have a monthly commitment to write at least one post. So, my faithful readers can expect to see that sustained no matter what. No matter how busy I get, there will always be a monthly blog post. That being said, I have been thinking about marriage lately (although it remains a constant feature in my sphere of thoughts), I am thinking about it more than ever before.

The more I think about it the more I question if truly I am ready for marriage. Yes, I have read a lot of books about marriage. I have attended many seminars and classes. I write and talk about marriage. In fact, I plan on turning my passion into a full-time career. But in spite of all these, when I truly consider the level of dependability that comes with signing that contract, I take a mental step back. Not because I don't want to be someone's helpmate but because I am not sure I am fully ready yet to be one.

I guess the bigger question here is, what does it take to be a helpmate? Maybe if we truly examine it, we will not demonstrate the eagerness toward marriage that many of us do. Perhaps the reason why marriages today are so turbulent is because we are signing up to help another person for the rest of our lives when we don't have a basic understanding of what it entails.

I always emphasize that a person cannot give what he or she doesn't have. Therefore, helping someone requires that you have what it takes to supply whatever need that person has, be it emotional, financial, spiritual, or physiological. We are consenting to helping the other person fulfill everything on Maslow's pyramid. That is what marriage is!

What ends up happening is that the moment of realization comes for many of us after we already took the vows not before. Then we get into this agreement called marriage and it dawns on us that we have really done the most sacrificial thing we could ever do, we have signed our lives away to the other person and we can't have it back. We are stuck for as long as we live. And as noble as that is, it is quite a responsibility.

But because we willingly decided to be with this person because of love, we don't think of the responsibility as burdensome. However, it is not enough to just love someone! We also must have what it takes to help the person. That's the first reason why marriage exists in the first place. God said in the garden of Eden, "I will make a helper suitable for him" and brought forth Eve. There would be no Eve, if Adam did not need a helper.

However, in this day and age, it is not enough for us women to be just women to decide that we have what it takes to help a man. Eve got away with it. But that's no longer applicable. It takes more than being beautiful or sexually attractive and many of us fail to grasp this. It takes wisdom, it takes being industrious, it takes financial acumen, it takes spiritual soundness, it takes a good heart and a bucket full of other qualities to be a helpmate!

Please get this right singles and married, the most assured way to make your marriage a success is to never stop developing yourself! Always pursue what makes you a better person, so you can increase your value and the value you bring to your relationship.

Self-improvement is a continuous process. But please don't get married until you have gotten to a very good place in your journey of self-betterment. That's the only way you could help another person, if you have first and foremost helped yourself.

CHAPTER 13: HEY LADIES! LET'S TALK SUBMISSION.

Over the years in my conversations with men, one thing I have come to realize is that submission is a really big deal to them. As a matter of fact, submission is such an important topic these days. More so in light of all the female empowerment movements and feminist movements happening in the media and society.

I am a feminist. I can't help but be one. I have been a feminist since I was a child, which is somewhat surprising considering my conservative upbringing. But my journey with feminism started in Nigeria, at a young age. I am an advocate for coining your own brand of feminism. I believe humans are too multifaceted for the restrictive labels society creates.

Marrying my Christian identity and my feminist identity has never been a conflict for me. To me one is not independent of the other. However, I understand it can be confusing for many Christian women out there, considering the somewhat subjugated role of women as laid down by Apostle Paul, which can be summarized by the word **Submission.**

Don't you just love that word? I believe submission is one of the most abused words that ever came out of the bible. But submission in marriage is really effortless when love is involved. Love makes it easy to submit. When spouses love each other, they are seeking to please each other in everything they do. As a wife your husband's wish becomes your command and your wish becomes his. The love for our spouse inspires our submission. Then submission does not need to be enforced because it comes from the heart.

According to the dictionary, "submission is the action or fact or accepting or yielding to a superior force or to the will or authority of another person." I mentioned earlier that while male and females are equal, for orderliness to exist, there has to be a hierarchy. In God's scheme of marriage, the man comes first. He has the higher authority. But remember marriage is a love affair? If there is true love, no man will be seeking to reassert his control or authority and no woman will be seeking to disobey or disrespect authority. Submission will become reciprocal, just like respect.

Couples will work and walk together in love. Besides, the same bible that instructs that wives submit, also states that husbands should honor their wives. I looked up the word *honor* and found many interesting synonyms including, obey, reverence, esteem, follow and respect.

However, I think it is crucial to marry a man whose authority you can submit to. If you consider a man not qualified enough to assert authority over you, please don't marry such a man! This is such a critical point. If we settle for a man who does not have the qualities that inspire our reverence, we will end up disrespecting our husbands. You don't want to get to a place where your husband no longer incite your admiration. Which is why we have to see beyond the looks and the money in making a decision. We have to examine the character of a man. Does he have leadership qualities? Can he lead me? Can he guide me? Does he have wisdom? Is he humble? Can I trust him? Is he dependable? What about this man just makes me want to yield to him? We have to consider all these factors!

If you get married to him, you have to submit. No matter how educated, wealthy, or enlightened we are as women, the moment we become wives, we become accountable to our husbands. That's just the way it is. We need to wrap our minds around it.

CONCLUSION

I was deeply moved by the sermon at the recent royal wedding between Prince Harry and Meghan Markle titled, "The Power of Love." The preacher started by reading from one the most romantic book that has ever been written, *The Song of Songs*. He read a particular passage that never fails to grab my attention every time I come across it. It reads, "Seat me as a seal upon your heart, set me as a seal upon your arm, **for** love is as strong as death, passion fierce as the grave, its flashes are flashes of fire, a raging flame. Many waters cannot quench love. Neither can floods drown it out." Songs of Solomon 8 verse 6. He then went on to say, "The late Dr. Martin Luther King once said, and I quote, we must discover the power of love, the redemptive power of love. And when we do that we will make of this old world a new world. The love, love is the only way." There's really nothing profound about what was said. It's been said countless times just how powerful love is that it has become a cliché. Yet it seems as though we have failed to grasp the implication of those words.

What jumps out to me the most from that *Song* are the words, "love is as strong as death." Remember at the beginning I mentioned what we have is a love problem, but I never quite defined what love is. The reason being that I haven't quite found a definition that encompasses all that love in. I doubt we could ever truly define love in succinct words. The best we could do is to draw a comparison like I did earlier when I likened love to gold. But the Bible uses an even stronger simile *death*.

It begs the question, why death? Why of all things is love likened to death? We all want love but arguably no one wants anything that has to do with death. They seem so far apart, a total antithesis of the other, but the wisest man who ever lived for reasons known to him chose to pair these two together. In an attempt to truly understand what the writer was trying to convey, I began comparing the two forces for similarities. The similarities are quite fascinating but the one I found most interesting is that death and love are equally the most powerful force in the universe, but while the power of death ends/dies here on earth, love reigns forever. There will come a time when death will no longer exist. But love transcends that time. It's not only the most powerful force here on earth; it will always be from everlasting to everlasting. When all else is gone love will remain, making it singularly the most powerful force *ever*. With love we can overcome any and every of life's obstacles as individuals and couples.

This gives me hope for every young person out there looking to get married and every couple out there struggling to make it work! If we don't give up on love, we can make our marriage all we desire for it to be!

And there you have it. My first book on marriage and relationships. This book is not all you need to have a great marriage, but it covers some really important basics. I have enjoyed writing this and hope to write more as a married woman. It would be interesting to see how my perspective has evolved. I look forward to a happy life and wish you the same. Thank you for reading!

www.ingramcontent.com/pod-product-compliance
Lightning Source LLC
LaVergne TN
LVHW051604070426
835507LV00021B/2750